The World Crisis
The Path to the World Afterwards

Europe and the World
in the decade from 2010 to 2020

By Franck Biancheri
Translated from French by Ian Shaw

ISBN 978-2-919574-00-1

I have written this book with my daughter Carla in mind, so that her world after the crisis should be better than the one before and Jean Guyot, whom I hope would have liked this book and who gave me so much support for my efforts that tomorrow is written in what was the best of yesterday.

I would like to thank Marie-Hélène for her unfailing support, our sometimes lively exchanges and her careful review, my parents and my friends Harald, Stéphane, Philippe and Frédéric for their insightful comments.

I would equally like to thank Eric Laurent who encouraged me to write this book, even if in the end the editorial process has been different to that which was expected.

Cannes/Dresden, October 2009 – February 2010

Four years before writing these pages, the 15th February 2006, I signed the first public announcement of the Laboratoire Européen d'Anticipation Politique (LEAP[1]), announcing the imminence of what I called « a global systemic crisis ».

Twenty years before, at the head of the first European students' forum, Aegee-Europe[2], I oversaw the adoption of the Erasmus programme, the famous European student mobility programme, which has so far allowed more than two million French, German, Polish, Dutch and other students to prepare to be the executives of an integrated Europe we have inherited from these last sixty years.

During this twenty year period a number of events took place which were the starting point for the historic crisis in which we now find ourselves.

By bringing together two decades of experience, acquired in France, Europe and globally since the '90s, and using the methods of political anticipation developed with LEAP, I have tried in this book to set out the principal characteristics of the world after the global crisis and to define some of the trends that will mark the 2010-2020 period.

Designed for ordinary citizens and policymakers alike, this book can be a useful tool to prepare for a decade which will mark an historic upheaval in the relations between major world regions. Whether you are a private citizen, running an association, local community or group, or business one thing is certain: the world-after that will emerge over the next ten years will bear little comparison to recent decades.

It is not unreasonable to assume that the current changes are the most important for the planet for over three centuries and the beginning of the conquest of the world by Europeans.

The years 2010-2020 will mark an historic transition of which the current crisis is the accelerator. Like any interim period between the world before the crisis and the one after, the next ten years bring a double destiny: opening the doors of a new global equilibrium, or alternatively plunging us deeper into international chaos. Twentieth century European history has already given us two examples of such periods of transition which could bring the worst as well as the best: the 1900s that led Europeans into the First World War and the 1920s and its missed opportunities which led straight to the Second World War in the next decade. It was particularly leaders' but also people's lack of imagination, preventing them from understanding how quickly their world was toppling into tragedy in the space of just a few years. History doesn't repeat itself. If, in lacking anticipation, we don't seize the

---

[2] European Students' Forum

opportunities which present themselves in an attempt to direct the course of history towards a better future, then the worst will become a certainty for us Europeans.

The decade that lies ahead of us undoubtedly belongs to this crucial category of major periods of historical transition.

The current crisis
is a global systemic crisis

The crisis thrusts us outside the world shaped by three centuries of European and Western domination

This time, as globalization requires, we are witnessing an upheaval of the world shaped for three centuries, first by the Europeans and subsequently by their extended family in the West (led by the United States).

In fact, proving the extent to which this crisis is unprecedented in modern history, the international system to which we are accustomed is witnessing an increasing number of events or trends emerging from age-old reference frames. The only way to evaluate the progression of events is to step back several centuries, the only measure now offering an adequate perspective. By limiting oneself to several decades' statistics, one only captures, in fact, the detail of this crisis not an overall view.

Let me give three examples showing that we live in a time of schism occurring only once every two or three centuries:

- In 2009, the Bank of England's base rate reached its lowest level (0.5%) since the creation of this venerable institution in 1694 (315 years of existence).

- In 2008, the Caisse des Dépôts, the financial arm of the French state since 1816 and under all regimes (monarchy, empire, republic, etc.), suffered its first annual loss (in 193 years).

- In April 2009, China became Brazil's largest trading partner, a relationship which for centuries has accurately forecast major disruption in global leadership. It is only the second time a country has achieved this since the United Kingdom ended three centuries of Portuguese hegemony two hundred years ago (the U.S. had, in fact, supplanted the United Kingdom in the early 1930s as Brazil's largest trading partner).

We are not going to dwell here on the increasing number of trends specific to the United States that emerge from national benchmarks of the last hundred years (earlier than that the country doesn't really have usable benchmarks for relevant comparison): fall in the value of the Dollar, public deficits, accumulated public debt, accumulated trade deficits, collapsing real estate market, financial institution losses, etc[3]. But of course, in the country at the heart of the global systemic crisis,

---

[3] Political leaders and experts continue to try and compare the current crisis to the 1929 crisis as if it were a bulletproof benchmark. However, in the United States in particular, current trends in many areas have

such examples are legion and now flourish in all the media, even the most "politically correct". Besides, it is this increase which is symptomatic of the leaving of the global reference frame. If one country or sector were affected, it would only be a matter of a period beyond the norm for that country or sector. But, today, there are many countries at the heart of the international system and numerous economic and financial sectors which are simultaneously affected by this "exit from the age-old path", by this systemic crisis that affects even the very mainstays of the world order we have known for decades, in fact for at least two to three centuries.

Let's take a simple example, this exit from longstanding reference frames takes the form of a curve, quite simply going off the chart that for centuries enabled the progression of the event or price in question to be represented. Moreover, the trend of exiting traditional reference frames is accelerating, affecting an increasingly significant number of sectors and countries. This event, then, automatically strengthens the loss of the signals used daily or monthly by the stock markets, governments, or statistical services[4] and accelerates the general awareness that the "usual signals" no longer allow an understanding of, nor even represent, current world developments. The planet therefore reaches the 2010-2020 decade without any reliable reference frame available.

Measuring the extent of the challenge posed for anticipating the world after the crisis

In order to clearly understand the problem that we all have in imagining the future, just spend a minute in the shoes of a Communist bloc country leader in 1985 who was asked to describe the situation in his country ten years hence[5]. How many of them could imagine (and tell) that ten years later their whole world (from a political, economic, social or cultural standpoint) would have disappeared[6] and a host of new questions (and answers), wholly unrelated to the Communist world,

---

exceeded those that characterized the "Great Depression". To find comparisons, we must now go and look for the benchmarks of the great world crisis of 1873-1879, more than a century ago.

[4] This explains in particular why everyone feels that official statistics diverge more and more from the everyday experience of life. In addition to their increasing manipulation by leaders who try to hide the truth that they have lost control, they have been created to describe a world that is disappearing a little more each day.

[5] Without even mentioning the ability of communist bloc statisticians to predict the economic and social developments in their countries for the next decade.

[6] In the knowledge that in their case, the model of society which was causing the collapse of their own (Western capitalist model) already existed, which is not the case anymore.

would invade their daily life: finding a job by oneself, coping with unemployment, paying for a whole host of previously free services (health, education, etc.), having the choice of living in their own country or going somewhere else, choosing their leaders, being able to disagree with their government, modeling themselves on the "opposing camp", etc. A tiny minority undoubtedly. In any case, certainly not the political, economic and intellectual elite of these countries, totally immersed in the vision of "their" world. However, ten years later, nothing remains of a world certain of its constancy, its values and its power (especially military), except socio-economic rubble.

Of course, like any analogy, this has its limitations, the main one being that the changes generated by the current global crisis are both much deeper and less dramatic than those initiated by the fall of the Berlin Wall in 1989. But, fundamentally, the nature of the process is the same. A historical crisis is, above all, a tremendous contraction of time: in a few years changes take place that are normally spread over decades or even centuries if the crisis is major. We are experiencing such a phenomenon at the moment. The world after this crisis will be profoundly different from that of these last few decades, or even two or three centuries. With the collapse of the U.S. cornerstone of world order created after 1945, it is, in fact, the central role of the West (Europe alone at first, then the Unites States and Europe jointly) disintegrating before our eyes closing a chapter on the history of the world which opened in the seventeenth century with the beginning of colonization. Thus, China and India which accounted for 50% of global GDP in the eighteenth century, are returning to centre stage, while Brazil and Russia assert their international role independently of the EU/USA duo, itself in full collapse. In the face of this historical breakdown Europeans must deal with a host of new collective and individual challenges: How to influence the developments of this "world after" from now on? How can Europe and the Europeans cope with the challenges of the world after the crisis? What kind of political leaders do we need to allow our country to come through the crisis successfully? What new socio-economic balances will the future bring? What risks of conflict will the coming decade bring? How to manage the heightened cultural diversity that will characterize the world after? What foreign languages should we teach our children in priority? Where to study? How to avoid losing investments and savings in these troubled times?

Just like the East Europeans had to suddenly learn that Moscow was no longer the center of the world[7], that studying Marx and Lenin no longer served any professional use, that speaking only Russian as a foreign language was no longer an asset in terms of employment, we are quickly going to have to reconsider our sources of information and ways of thinking to understand the new global power

---

[7] And gradually discovering that Brussels was going to influence their daily lives as they knew nothing or almost nothing of the European Community.

relationships and the resulting developments and we will have to learn to communicate with cultures that seemed delightfully exotic to us a short time ago. Think of the Volvo workers who suddenly discovered in December 2009 that their bosses would be Chinese from therein on and no longer American. No doubt the career prospects at Volvo have now led to a real mental revolution among its employees regarding the relative importance of Beijing and Washington, Chinese and English. In a way, we have all become 1985 Eastern Europeans working for Volvo!

Thus, the pages that follow, particularly inspired by the work of the European Laboratory of Political Anticipation (LEAP) and the Europe2020[8] network where I have directed research for many years, are an attempt to discern the major trends that will shape the world in the next ten years to help each of us to make the best choices for our lives and those of our children. Because to anticipate the future only makes sense if one can learn the lessons and arrive at the decisions to take today.

With this book, the path over the next ten years I have finally chosen to explore includes three major phases: a presentation of the trends at work in the global crisis and their implications, particularly for France, "windows" on certain developments for which each of us can prepare and act, and finally two accounts of the future, two scenarios for 2010-2020, which aim to "flesh out" the two major alternatives offered to the world in the next ten years[9]. These are two alternative histories of the future, showing the likely chain of possible events in case the international community (and, therefore, each of us) will try to prepare for the world after the crisis or, on the contrary, attempt to save the world before at any price.

So, en route to the world after!

The present depends as much on our experiences as our expectations

One last comment before we start.

Our relationship with the future has fundamentally changed in the space of fifty years. I do not think that history should be explained by a system of ideological, religious or scientific thought. It only acquires its coherence once dead and only in our own eyes, for us, who live in the present and are fickle. Anticipating the future

---

[8] LEAP and the Europe 2020 network especially are the originators of the concept of "global systemic crisis" to describe the current crisis that they had correctly anticipated since February 2006. For more information on this subject, it is possible to consult a large number of publications at www.leap2020.eu.

[9] It is not, of course, a case of predicting future events, but an attempt to improve the accuracy of trends and conceptual analyses so as to better understand what they represent, translated by "past history", when events are frozen in the past.

can, therefore, only be an attempt to identify major trends which are becoming apparent and the constants they generate. The latter will take shape as the inevitable elements of the next few years, predictable examples between which the elusive fluidity of time will slide. The trends at work constitute the forces that, when they hit the wall of the present, hasten events[10]. These events, which form the fabric of what we call history, are only, in fact, "dead" historical trends, precipitated by their contact with what was yesterday.

However, these trends are also active in the future. Our era is, moreover, perhaps the first to emphasize this reality, the future now has as much influence as the past on present-day society. Indeed, until the mid-twentieth century, humanity has largely determined what it does based on habits, traditions and past actions. We followed in our fathers' footsteps. We used the « right tools » which our ancestors bequeathed us and thus it always was, yesterday shaped today. And yet a widespread change has come about in several decades. Indeed, who today would use the computer left to him by his father? Or the phone? Or even the central heating boiler, taking climate change into account? It is our anticipation of the next constituent parts in the making, or standard requirements, or climate change which determine our choices. From now on its tomorrow which decides today for us.

If the speed of technological change is certainly an essential factor in this development, it isn't the only one. The dizzying growth of the world population in a few decades is, in effect, strongly linked to the direct influence of the future on the present, especially in human activity having a significant impact on the planet and its development (climate change, nuclear waste, expansion of the deserts, etc.) from now on. At the same time the growth of political entities in populations of many hundreds of millions of inhabitants (the European Union, the United States, etc.), even exceeding a billion inhabitants (China, India) is radically changing world geopolitics: one changes from umpiring a sailing regatta to the management of fleets of super tankers. Suffice it to say here, in this case too, anticipation and the idea we have of the future become: a necessity: one doesn't change a super tanker's course like a sailing boat's. One must be able to plan the changes in course hours, even days, ahead. Forces of inertia require anticipation.

Thus, one discovers that last feature of our real world which has contributed to alter our relationship with the times[11]: its complexity. Modern society has become so crowded and complex that the only way of solving a problem is, henceforth, to succeed in stopping it happening, otherwise the interplay at the heart of the complexity of our society causes unexpected blockages and consequences which

---

[10] As a chemical reaction precipitates solids from liquids.

[11] For the sake of completeness, it is necessary to add the increase in life expectancy to these features. As an example, a century ago, twenty years was half the average lifespan, whereas it is now a quarter.

generally lead to worsening problems. The attempts to resolve the current world crisis are good examples: in order to save world finance the majority of the leading States have been put in a catastrophic budgetary position. One sees, therefore, how and why from now on history will be written in the future as much as the past because, more than ever, our current decisions are as much the result of our past experiences as our anticipations. However, today in the world, our elite, our leaders (without even, of course, speaking of the people in general) are just not trained in this new form of history. Nowhere[12] have they been taught to anticipate in order to lead, whilst what was wise advice for skilful leaders has become a vital need for the whole of humanity.

Taking stock of the current crisis, a global systemic crisis

First, let's dwell on the current situation for a moment because before taking the road, we should really know our starting point and what the weather conditions are. In this case, let's quickly analyze the nature of the crisis because it profoundly determines tomorrow's trends. This crisis is still ongoing and is therefore part of the next decade's landscape. It is, of course, global in the sense that it simultaneously affects all countries of the world and all sectors of human activity. It is systemic because it affects the very foundations of the world we have known for many decades, even for two or three centuries.

The crisis is pre-eminently global. Indeed, no country is immune. The U.S. is the epicenter. It was the « subprime » mortgage crisis of 2006 that triggered the collapse of Wall Street in October 2008, leading the entire global financial system into an unprecedented panic and forcing the central banks of all the major economic powers to flood the planet with liquidity to avoid a widespread banking collapse. The « black hole » into which this liquidity has been poured (and continues to be) represents between 20 and 30 trillion USD of « ghost-assets », that is to say assets that, in fact, were never worth what the markets priced them at before the crisis. These are houses whose prices have been slashed in half or by two thirds, empty business premises that no one wants to rent or buy, shares of financial institutions whose value has fallen by 90% in two years, shares of bankrupt companies (like GM or Lehman Brothers), constantly falling currencies (like the U.S. Dollar or the Pound), the bonds of increasingly indebted States which nobody wants (California, Dubai, Greece). And we're only half way along the path;

---

[12] At LEAP, for the last year we have started to bring political anticipation to the universities. But it's a drop of water in the face of the need to train tens of thousands of leaders and public sector and private executives.

there is still certainly half of these impaired assets which remain to be accounted for, either by banks, States or individuals:

- The business centres of cities like Paris, London, Amsterdam, New York, etc. are gathering an increasing number of empty buildings every day that nobody buys or rents, and of which the owners (often banks and insurance companies) will have to greatly reduce the prices between now and the end of 2010.

- U.S. housing has failed to stop falling, despite the unprecedented financial efforts of the Federal Reserve to try to lower mortgage interest rates and the Obama Administration to encourage buyers (8,000 Dollar tax credit). A fall in average prices of about 20% to 30% between now and 2011 is still likely. In France (particularly in the Parisian and Cote d'Azur "bubbles"), as in the United Kingdom or Spain, the situation is the same. Owners will be required to comply with the demands of buyers who have fled the market and still haven't returned.

- The dollar, pillar of the entire world monetary system since 1945 and so "a benchmark measure of the value of the global economy" continues to fall against all major currencies in the world (Euro, Yen, Real and, soon, the Yuan which will have to be revalued whether the Chinese government likes it or not: we will come back to this later), consequently contributing to the depreciation of all Dollar denominated assets (U.S. Treasury Bonds, shares of U.S. companies, etc.).

- The value of U.S. Government Treasury Bonds (the principal financial instrument used as reserves by many central banks around the world, including the Chinese, Japanese and oil producing nations' central banks) is increasingly uncertain due to the twin events of a staggering increase in the amount issued (2 trillion USD forecast for 2010) to finance U.S. public deficits which are growing exponentially and due to manipulation of their value (via interest rates) by the Federal Reserve itself. Their true value is probably around 50% of current "market" prices. And they are not the only government securities to lose value! British "Gilts" are following the same path, Japanese bonds too! As for the rise in public deficits in France and Germany, it leads to a growing loss of confidence in the bonds they issue.

The recovery that can't happen

2010 was also marked by widespread awareness that the long awaited "recovery" announced in 2009 by Western and Chinese political and financial leaders not having materialized, public deficits and, therefore, Government bonds are the new "subprime bubble". This time, it will not be a matter of insolvent households but insolvent States and the consequences that will materialize during the decade will be infinitely more serious. For there to be a "recovery" business investment, consumer spending, or exports would, in fact, have to take off again to take over from huge public spending in 2009. Now we see all around us that the consumer has become permanently thrifty (or insolvent due to massive unemployment or unmanageable debt), that all countries want to export (which obviously makes an export-led recovery impossible because importers are needed for that to work[13]) and that, consequently, no responsible businessman would make any significant investments in absence of any commercial prospects.

The West is committing suicide
with the new bubble in Government borrowing

The major geopolitical characteristic of this bubble in state borrowing is that, unlike previous crises, it is the West, and especially the United States and the United Kingdom, which is now bankrupt. It is, then, the heart of the global system which is suffering from an embolism. This helps to illustrate the systemic nature of the crisis. Indeed, when the peripheral players are affected (such as during the 1997 Asian crisis for example), the global system itself can manage the problem with little risk to its performance. But when countries at the heart of the global system are severely affected, the entire global mechanism is affected, even beyond financial, economic and monetary circles. To try to "save itself" the United States is obliged to increasingly bend the rules of the game, and condemned to yield to the demands of other players, even when they are contrary to the long-term interests of the existing system. Clearly, now in a position of suppliants vis-à-vis most of the world, especially powers in direct competition like China or Russia, the United States and their faithful British lieutenant must gradually cede control of the system and thus ultimately the system itself since it was built by them for themselves.

Certainly the G20's inability to act effectively is a consequence of the reluctance of the United States to cede control of global governance, but the very existence of the G20 as a new, privileged inner sanctum to discuss this global governance (and the recognized end of the G7 in the affair) shows, as far as it is concerned, the end of the West's monopoly (United States and European satellite countries) over this same global governance. 2009 will, without doubt, be remembered as the year of the beginning of the effective transition to a new world

---

[13] Here, the United States, like the EU, will quickly understand that China is absolutely not counting on playing the role of "saviour" of Western economies. Instead of encouraging them by imports generated by its growth, Beijing intends to use the latter to perpetuate an Asian bloc around China. The Chinese authorities have thus ordered businesses in the country to systematically favour Asian suppliers to the detriment of American and European ones.

order, but it is the beginning of a transition, as was the creation of the League of Nations after the First World War[14] or the UN after the Second World War. The next decade will declare to which category the current transition belongs: to that which succeeds in giving birth to a relatively stable and lasting world order, or to that which leads straight to an even more violent crisis.

In this sense, the failure of the Copenhagen summit on global warming is only an example of the ongoing transition between the world before and the world after the crisis. On the one hand, the question of growing planetary pollution is an illustration of the impasse in which the Western views of socio-economic development find themselves which in practice could only be an elitist development, restricted to a « rich man's club » in total contradiction, therefore, with the democratic principles displayed by the West in political affairs. On the other hand, the inability of the same West to develop a common strategy to try to lead the entire planet in the direction it wanted reveals the growing rift between its two American and European elements. The United States does not want strong environmental constraints because its economy is closer to that of an emerging country like China or India than those of European countries. Finally, the failure of the Copenhagen summit is also an example of the inability of European leaders to understand that Washington is no longer part of the solution but really part of the problem and it is, from now on, in spending time and energy on Moscow, Beijing, New Delhi or Brasilia that Europe can effectively influence major global developments. With the European elite fed on « Washington's tit », it is evidently a major challenge[15], similar to the one Eastern Europe had to face after 1989, where all its elite had a « Muscovite wet nurse ».

Yet a crisis is only a time of particularly savage adjustment. It is not necessarily a negative experience for everyone. On the contrary even, some come out winners. For this reason we should keep in mind that moral judgments on the current crisis must be put into perspective. Some trends are, in fact, negative for most people around the world, but not others. Either certain sections thrive while others are in despair, or some countries become stronger while others collapse. In short, the world after will clearly see the winners and losers and this is inevitable. What is avoidable, on the other hand, and where Europe can play a key role, is that it

---

[14] An illustration of one of the setbacks of the lost decade of transition of the 1920s. The inability of the G20 to act on the key issues is likely to make it quickly look like an early modern equivalent of the League of Nations. It took a new decade and a world war to culminate in the UN system that contributed to the stability of the following decades.

[15] This question of the kind of elite needed by tomorrow's Europe will, of course, be discussed in detail in a chapter of this book; as will the impact of China, India and Russia's big comeback on the forefront of the world stage and the emergence of new powers like Brazil.

should be a zero sum game and that those who have losses in one area should not have gains in another. Hence the importance of the next decade, which will mould the conditions for progress towards the world after the crisis.

2010-2020
Build a new global governance or gradually sink into a conflict between major regional blocs

The decade 2010 - 2020
The lynchpin of world order for the following decades

If we add the continuing population explosion to these factors, which will take world population to about eight billion people between now and 2020 and its inevitable tragic consequences (about which much has been written) in terms of food, water, flight to the cities, pollution, epidemics and therefore conflicts of all kinds, the scene has been set to identify the major trends that will shape the world after the global crisis in the 2010-2020 decade.

Let's also bear in mind that this decade will shape the world's leaders of the period 2020-2030 as well as their base of political legitimacy. It is, then, doubly crucial. On the one hand, because it's the decade for managing the crisis and, on the other, because it will shape the world's consciousness differently for the next decade according to which it will bequeath it a legacy of lasting world order in the process of early development or unmanageable chaos. This can be called a "lynchpin decade", a sort of switch that will directly determine the path that world history will take for the following decades. Each one of us, citizen or leader, must take special care to understand the issues and try to anticipate the possible and probable developments in order to act for the best now.

One of this decade's characteristics is that it marks the first major change in world leadership in a closed and densely populated world. During the handover from Britain to the U.S. in the 1930s, the world had just finished being explored, different civilizations still "saw" little of each other and there were still traces of virgin territory. Today, all that has ended, the world is closed and full to bursting. As to the different civilizations, they mingle with growing promiscuity bringing well-chosen crossbreeding as well as violent xenophobia. The historical context of the last handover will also lead us into error if we want to believe in an analogy with the decade that is just beginning, at least keep in mind that, even if the transmission of world leadership took place peacefully between the United Kingdom and the United States, it was organized against a backdrop of two world wars.

When there is a change of governance of the planet, a whole series of players think they have the right to try their luck - that applies from the local separatist movement, to regional powers via various fundamentalist religious groups. The longer the interregnum, the longer yesterday's world takes time to disappear with more lasting violence and brutality pervading the same period. That is really the great danger lurking at the heart of the decade which is just beginning, failing to give birth to the world of the future and extend a turbulent era for a decade longer.

The inability of the G20 to change the international game in 2009 leads to inevitable global geopolitical dislocation

The inability of the G20 summits in late 2008 and 2009 to address the central issue of current global governance (i.e., the role of the U.S. Dollar as the international benchmark currency) has initiated a process of global geopolitical dislocation which will be the dominant trend of the 2010-2020 decade. The choice which was offered to world leaders in 2009 was not between resolving the crisis or not resolving it, it was between managing the crisis in such a way as to limit its duration and negative impact, or really let the world be engulfed by the crisis and its consequences. In the first case, one could expect an exit from the crisis in three to five years from now (probably somewhat longer for the United States and the United Kingdom). In the second case, a long period of at least a decade (certainly much more for the United States and the United Kingdom) of widespread global instability (political, economic, social and strategic) is set in motion.

This may seem paradoxical given the respective complexities of the crisis and the contemporary world, but the crux of the problem is actually of childlike simplicity. A little over sixty years ago, world balance of power consisted of a global superpower in its death throes, the United Kingdom, and a superpower in the phase of rapidly moving up in the world, the United States. Both players decided to join forces to maximize their upside gains (the American case) and minimize their downside losses (the British case). The rest of the world was either under colonial control, or too impoverished by the Second World War to really influence events. Only Stalin's Russia could exert any influence, albeit very limited because of its economic weakness and the archaic way it operated. Very quickly, unable to compete on equal terms, it refused to « play ball » with the other powers and embarked on its own game in a closed environment, the « communist bloc »[16]. Little by little, the rest of the world organized itself around the American player, in whose shadow the British player gradually weakened. The dominant player's currency and economy became the benchmarks for the whole planet. In 1989 the Soviet player began to implode and, from the early 1990s, the world game only had one major player, the United States.

However, this prominent development hid two others which were less obvious to discern. After 50 years during which part of the world had been cut out of the global game, the game became the same for the whole world. So, it had expanded, automatically diluting certain key factors such as the standing of the dominant player relative to its population, economy, influence, etc. On the other hand, an accompanying quickening in technology (satellite, internet, transport, etc.) has

---

[16] It was powerful enough to create its own game, but not to hope to play the game imposed by the United States and the United Kingdom on equal terms.

increased the stature of certain players at the heart of what one has begun to call «globalization».

This last phenomenon contributed to sharply put into context the stature of the dominant player in the whole of the game. However, the dominant player's privileged role and its attributes (currency, economy, etc.) had nothing to do with a «clear destiny», a cultural superiority or some purpose of history, but rather everything to do with the conditions at the origin of the global system as it was founded in 1945. In 1945, the United States was almost the game on its own, possessing more than 50% of global industry and holding 90% of the world's gold reserves at a time when gold was the basis of the international monetary system. It was both the world's banker and its factory. It was the game and its currency, the Dollar, its favorite tool. It was THE player!

Thus, one would think that the problem that confronted the world in 1945 to rebuild a stable international system after the destruction of the previous one by two successive world wars was very simple. How to develop a game that the player likes? How to ensure that THE player really wants to play (to trade, finance, supply, produce, etc.) with other players? It's the answer to this question which founded the whole system we inherited in 1945.

On April 2, 2009, during the G20 summit in London, world leaders should have been aware that they were no longer confronting an issue of this sort at all. For the reasons briefly outlined above, there is no longer a dominant player and secondary players, even insignificant ones (whereas that really was the case in 1945). Now there are several major players. So that the game works (to trade, finance, supply, produce, etc.), the world needs these several key players to really want to play. And for this to happen, it is necessary that the game, its purpose, rules and apparatus suits them, otherwise a number of them will refuse to play in the knowledge that, today, such a situation would mark a profound and lasting crisis of the world's entire political economic, financial and commercial system.

It is this aspiration of the important new players that is recognized in the demand of China, Brazil or Russia to have more say at the International Monetary Fund before making any new capital contributions, or in that of the EU (and the Eurozone in particular) to see a radical reform of the rules controlling the global financial system before considering any new economic stimulus as requested by Washington. And if the G20 has emerged as a central player in recent months at the expense of Washington alone, the American-British pair, or the G7, it is quite simply because this change is building a little more every day, like an incontrovertible pressure, to try to stem the current crisis.

And as with any new product in the world where "at the beginning there was something very specific", in the modern world economy and world trade, like Bretton Woods in 1944, "at the beginning there was the international benchmark currency". The difference is that at Bretton Woods, a discussion really took place which was logically[17]decided in favor of the Dollar. Whilst at the G20, for now, everyone is talking about anything but that.

However, that really is the key to the problem. The nature of the benchmark international currency defines the game. If it is the currency of a single player, then there is THE player and the others are secondary. If it is a basket of currencies, then there are THE players (those whose currencies make up the basket of currencies) and there are the others. From this rule (several major players) and this instrument (a common benchmark currency), everything else follows: the stability of the currency markets, commodity prices including oil, regulation of financial markets, etc. and, ultimately, global stability because each of the major players now has a vested interest in playing the game, a game in which they can predict the courses of action and their consequences, a requirement sine qua non for a long lasting game.

If, despite the evidence, the G20 is unable to change the game, because the current player refuses and/or through lack of courage or confidence on the part of major new players, then, in front of the persistence of current imbalances (increasing instability in currency markets, unpredictable changes in commodity prices, increasing danger in financial markets, deepening social crises, etc.), every major player will begin to do what Stalin's USSR did in 1949. Unable to play on equal terms, unable to predict its courses of action and their consequences, every big player will refuse to play the "rigged big game" and create its own "small game", faction, sector of influence[18], and will let political, economic or military head-on impacts decide relations with other factions. These impacts will ultimately be seen as more predictable by each big player than a game rigged in favour of just one major player.

Modern history has, unfortunately, taught that this alternative will end tragically. But that same history has, unfortunately, a tendency not to offer many opportunities. The G20 missed its chance in 2009, so the 2010-2014 period will see each player of influence trying to shape the future global game according to its own interests beginning, in particular, by defining a new benchmark international currency instead of the Dollar[19]. If several players of influence, constituting a large enough geopolitical critical mass, reach agreement between now and 2014 on the broad guidelines of this twenty-first century global governance, then the second half of the decade will be marked by the gradual and essentially peaceful

---

[17] Considering the conditions of the game's creation.

[18] The United States will obviously follow this trend too.

[19] Unlike the Euro, which is a tangible currency, such an international benchmark currency would only exist electronically, first as a unit of account, secondly for trade between states and very large economic entities. There would be no wish to replace a particular currency.

establishment of this "new world order[20]". However, if such a convergence is not achieved, either through the spinelessness of some political players such as the Eurozone (and particularly France) or hardline confrontation between other key players (such as the United States and China), then the second half of the decade will unfortunately be the battleground of a series of violent clashes, economic and trade in particular, doomed to tragically lead to the new twenty-first century geopolitical balance for which the following decade will provide a bloody arena.

Two major trends will steer the 2010-2020 decade

It is this central issue that will separate the 2010-2020 decade into two parts. The period 2010/2014, which could be described as end of the « world before », will be essentially characterized by the continuation and deepening of the global systemic crisis. The 2015/2020 period will coincide with the tangible emergence of the « world after » the crisis. So that the new can be born, the former must really be dead. However, these two periods are not separated by distinct intervals; they will be marked by continuing events as well as by disruptions. Simply, the first part will be characterized primarily by events marking the end of the world order we knew until the 2000s, while the 2015-2020 will be the preferred period for putting the foundations of the new post-crisis global order in place, or even a new world disorder conducive to large-scale military conflict.

The two narratives of the decade presented at the end of this book are an attempt to show clearly the two possible faces of the next decade, depending on whether the players' efforts to try to bring the world after the crisis to the fore between now and 2020 will be successful or that, on the contrary, the strength of the players wishing to preserve the "world before" will prevent this development: the first scenario is called "The harrowing dawn of the world after", the other "The tragic twilight of the world before".

In both scenarios, there are identical events corresponding to what may be termed "invariants", that is to say the inevitable trend for the decade ahead. These invariants are also the subject of "windows", small chapters assigned to certain indisputable trends of the next ten years, which consequently are also events for which one can prepare, either to protect oneself or, on the other hand, to benefit from them.

---

[20] Far from the same concept that G. Bush Sr. imagined in 1991, when it had to be based on the central power of the United States alone.

For example, European integration is one of these invariants, while the ability of European nations and nationals to influence world history isn't. Indeed, this decade will mark a turning point for the history of our countries and our people. At a time when the major geopolitical groups which will shape the twenty-first century (these supertankers mentioned above) are forming up, time is running out for European nations who will quickly have to choose their future. And they have a great chance if they want to take it: after more than 60 years in the shadows, Europe again becomes a key player in global geopolitical developments.

The French case: The French and France at the crossroads
Influence history again or sink into anonymity

If the attitude of the Sino-American duo determines the extent to which chaos reigns in the first part of the next decade, Europeans will be primarily responsible for the stability or instability of the second half the decade and thus for much of the twenty-first century. The French, as key European players, will have to choose whether they want to again make history or whether they are content to be passive and anonymous subjects. Help the birth of the future or cling to the past, this could be a good definition of the option available to the French between now and 2020.

Because for us, Europeans and French, there is indeed a choice to make. And it is certainly a big novelty for us because, since the Second World War, we have no longer had a say on the world's main direction. In France, only De Gaulle has been able to achieve a certain amount of independent international influence for the country. Giscard and Mitterrand were only able to do so at European level while Chirac, rather by chance, once again succeeded in playing in the big league thanks to his unlikely pairing with Schroeder. In Sarkozy's hands, France's voice has purely and simply disappeared[21] and the country has taken a back seat in America's shadow, in even deeper shade than the United Kingdom (which is saying something).

However, the era opened up by the crisis is unprecedented, Europe is unified and no longer really has a master, except that which it chooses for itself. This is, incidentally, the current drama. The United States is no longer able to dominate the EU, but our leaders have chosen to behave as minions. What is true for most EU Member States is definitely the case for France. Faced with the possibility of making significant choices, it confines itself to obey and even preempt the wishes of a master which no longer has any power. "We are entering an epic epoch yet our leaders have nothing epic anymore", to paraphrase Léo Ferré.

---

[21] The trend lurking at the heart of this decade which is the great danger for us French is already at work. Current foreign policy is causing our slide into anonymity. We are starting to become a mere footnote on the pages written by Washington.

The United States is struggling with a moribund economy, staggering debt, a sliding currency, two military stalemates and a population 30% less than the EU's, but the EU continues to obey it as in the middle of the 1950s, when it was divided, under the heel of two military superpowers, and impoverished by two world wars in less than a generation. Worse still, while France in that situation, however difficult, produced a leader like de Gaulle, now it can only devote itself to being a Washington parrot. From one end of Europe to the other, as well as the world, the French are being watched with amazement and sadness. At the very moment when several decades of French efforts to exist independently and once again have an impact on the running of the world are, thanks to European integration, finally being successful, we drop the prey for the shadows, power for submission, leadership for blind conformity. Many people conjure up an image of Petain when looking at present-day France and they are not wrong. Submission to the strongest, negative view of national identity (compared to such and such), inability to think of Europe positively ("we're against it"), powerful rhetoric and an attitude of helplessness, etc. There are numerous similarities.

As is often the case in France's history, we are allowed to hear politely that we are incapable of steady effort. Incidentally, this was the British view of our country in the nineteenth century which criticized its cowardly side preventing it from rising to its full potential. Napoleon and de Gaulle shared another, namely that the big difference between the United Kingdom and France was that the British elite were in the front-rank despite a somewhat unsophisticated people, whereas if the French people were at the forefront, its elite, on the other hand, were at the back. We will see that France's current situation in the face of the world's challenges after the crisis fits perfectly with this dual Napoleonic and Gaullist definition.

Because he who says an historic choice is possible, says that a tough decision has to be taken. The recent episode of the policy of vaccination against Swine Fever during the course of which the French "decision-makers" hid behind the experts to ultimately have ridicule heaped upon them because of their disproportionate, inefficient and expensive plan clearly illustrates the situation. Leaders who do not even dare follow their common sense for fear of being held responsible for a problem are not adapted to a decade of historic choices because, by definition, they are not the choices of experts or consultants[22] but the choice of leaders, of bosses, thus implying a heavy political and historical responsibility. To be right, one must take the risk of being wrong. Otherwise one doesn't aspire to a leadership role.

Swine Fever has at least demonstrated that France wasn't run by decision-makers, but only advised by an army of consultants. This is not good news for addressing this crucial decade for the world order. Especially as France's standing in Europe directly determines the ability of Europe to be able to best deal with the

---

[22] Consultants are paid to take orders, not risks

challenges of the next decade itself. To cross from one world order to another is not an easy challenge and the oldest and most important member states in demographic and economic terms will be decisive in shaping the post-crisis European strategy. France, by itself and by its crucial pairing with Germany at the heart of the European process will be a key component. Now there will be no vision of France in the "world-after-the-crisis" that will not be intimately linked to a vision of Europe in the "world-after-the-crisis".

This is, moreover, very much the belief of the Americanist elite who want Europe to dissolve into an all-embracing West, centered on the United States and determined by its fight against various forces of evil (terrorists, global warming, Swine fever, etc.) and who, then, have set about shaping the French view on this particular plan. Only the superannuated Gallic alter-fundamentalists persist in claiming that they have a vision of France in tomorrow's world that is not intimately linked to a vision of Europe in the future. Alas, apart from being anti-everything or almost, none of them has been able to define what influence this proud France would have, lonely as a Transat racing yacht with its 65 million inhabitants, in a world where supertankers with 300 million to 1.5 billion inhabitants cruise. Without them realizing it, their lack of realism exactly serves the cause of those who want to make a clean sweep of the fundamental successes of after 1945, that's to say the programme of the National Council of the Resistance[23] and European integration, two of the key assets for France and Europe to meet the crisis first of all, and then to shape the world after the crisis. Make no mistake, a component of the current crisis is the fall of the other half of the Iron Curtain. In 1989, the fall of the Berlin Wall triggered the collapse of the Eastern part, the one built by the USSR. Today, following the collapse of Wall Street (it's obviously a story of a Wall), by « pulling the rug » from underneath the Dollar, we are seeing the other part collapsing in front of our very eyes.

Europeans are the only possible switchmen for the world train between 2010 and 2020

Thus, some of the strengths and stakes that one finds, in Europe in any case, to define the world of tomorrow comes directly from this past dating from before the Second World War. The Nazis also had a vision of Europe and the world, and there were many who shared it in France, Italy, Spain, Hungary, Romania, etc., a vision embodied in a West in conflict with everything that it wasn't. If you watch the television and read newspapers, you will inevitably find this image surprisingly up-to-date.

---

[23] And its equivalents put into place in the majority of the Western European countries after 1945, namely universal social security, independence of the media, free high-standard education, etc.

This book, then, also follows the example of a useful piece of advice for any traveler preparing for a difficult new route: don't overlook the experience of those who, in the past, have had to face the same, who have had to rebuild a new world order on the ruins of the former. Not to copy them, because history does not repeat itself, but to fully appreciate the extent of the difficulties and the characteristics of recurring dangers. Well, if any political entity is a past master on the subject, it is the European Union, hence the Europeans' special responsibility in this transition between two worlds. This book is, of course, written from a European point of view. Let us not forget that the same events could be characterized differently if one is American, Chinese or Brazilian.

Finally some clarification on this French and European point of view. Being French in Europe in the early twenty-first century is a kind of curse[24] because the other Europeans are waiting for us to play a leading role and, at the same time, are always ready to dismiss us if it's convenient. A seemingly untenable situation, but only in appearance, because with the time and experience of managing European teams and projects, one learns the possibilities and limitations of this French status in the midst of other Europeans: initiating without imposing, leading without ordering, testing before suggesting, lasting rather than going up in flames. The British know how to laugh at themselves. Here is an exercise, difficult for someone French, yet allowing one to slip into the shoes of a twenty-first century French European. Those who succeed discover the unique potential offered by a European team.

In order to function in Washington as well as Moscow, in front of Asians or Latin Americans, a quality European team is simply irresistible at world level. No team in the world today can really make the weight against well organized and determined Europeans. This is, moreover, what really worries Washington[25] whose language is only intended to make Europeans doubt themselves, and whose only ambition is to put incompetents and yes-men at their head. And it is really this that the Chinese, Russians, Indians and Brazilians hope and fear at the same time and who expect the Europeans to help them « softly » swing yesterday's world to the world of tomorrow. That is just one of Europeans' skills at the beginning of the twenty-first century. Unlike the prattle coming from the failed generation (the one in power today and which has known neither war, nor Europe, but only the perpetual adolescence of the 60s and 70s), a European team doesn't know how to win against its opponents, it knows how to win with them. This is the constraint imposed by a limited world, densely populated, with scarce resources and with the

---

[24] Although far less dramatic than being German and having to constantly refuse to exercise any leadership.

[25] By Washington, I mean here the players who wield the real power in the United States, that's to say primarily Wall Street, corporate America and the military. Unlike these players, in general the American citizen is really quite open to the idea of sharing the burden of global governance with other people, especially with Europeans.

means of infinite destruction. No game is won anymore against the opponent; no war is won by direct conflict.

Here, it is essential to keep in mind that one of the main reasons why the world will have a choice between a tragic or painful path during the next decade is the existence of nuclear weapons. Indeed, if the United States, Russia, China and Europe (via France and the United Kingdom) didn't have nuclear weapons, it is likely that the crisis would have already led to serious military tensions , of "gunboat diplomacy" aiming to increasingly unblock business or customs duties, numerous military adventures of which Afghanistan and Iraq are but pale versions. The assurance that every adventure of this sort will end in very deadly conflicts in which the elite itself may perish currently guarantees that the military option is not on the menu for direct interaction between major powers.

Fortunately Barack Obama's rantings on a nuclear-free world are totally unrealistic[26] because if they were borne out, they would overcome the main hurdle that prevented a new world war for over sixty years. There really is a major global problem in the nuclear field and the next decade will finally have to deal with it, but it is neither denuclearization (unrealistic and dangerous) nor non-proliferation (ineffective and dangerous as seen with Iran). It is a matter of controlled dissemination, or how to organize the transition from a closed nuclear club claiming to control the world on nuclear affairs when it hasn't controlled anything for at least two decades, to a system allowing the guarantee of peaceful regional balances through the supervised possession of nuclear weapons. The shortest path in politics is never a straight line, and even more so in geopolitics.

If it really is inevitable that the "world after" will see winners and losers what is avoidable, on the other hand, is that it should be a zero sum game. We must ensure in some way that those who lose in one domain are compensated elsewhere. It is, therefore, certain that the transition from the world before to the world after the crisis will be played out on the recognition or not by the major global players that one does not win against, but with, the other powers. If this new pressure is progressively integrated into the strategy of each of the G20 powers then, between now and the end of the decade, we will be collectively in the process of building the new world order for the twenty-first century. The Europeans have a particular role, to do everything in order that this pressure, which they well know, should be clearly identified by all. The path will certainly be painful, because giving birth to the future always happens with the pain of unemployment, financial losses, social and political unrest, ending of privileges, etc. But the process will avoid the most savage conflicts and especially prevent the transition dragging on without leading

---

[26] It's a joke seeing the president of a country unable to control the proliferation of firearms on its own territory claiming to organize non-proliferation of weapons globally. In politics actions speak louder than words.

to even greater chaos. It is this "harrowing dawn of the world after" that I try to graphically present in the 2010-2020 timeframe of the same name.

However, if we fail to make every major international player recognize (as was already the case throughout 2009, from the G20 London Summit to that in Copenhagen on global warming) that there is no way of winning against the others, then we will embark the whole planet on a tragic path mapped out on the 2010-2020 timeframe called the "the tragic twilight of the world before". Far from creating the infrastructure for a lasting new world order between now and 2020, this decade will only have been one long slide into a period of direct and violent conflicts between the major global powers.

The first half of the decade marked primarily by world geopolitical dislocation

The crisis, because it wasn't anticipated by world leaders, is advancing at its own speed. In 2009 the financial efforts, without historical precedent, of the United States, Europe, China, Japan and other countries have allowed only two things to happen: to anesthetize the general population in various countries in order to postpone a violent political and social reaction and to save the major financial institutions without reforming them. All that done at the cost of an intolerable State debt burden, the conversion of a very large part (around 30%) of the world economy into a "zombie economy" (that's to say surviving only through direct or indirect state aid or even via the manipulation of accounting rules) and a growing distrust of Western public opinion vis-à-vis all the ruling classes rightly suspected of being no more than the representatives of the most powerful financial interests. Alongside these very visible events, and ultimately in the short or medium term, the crisis represents other secular trends profoundly changing the world order we know, in particular China and India's return to power and the end of a Western-centric world.

The decade now dawning will be the setting for the interaction between these two "stages" of the crisis which, whilst being correlated of course, are not identical. The secular trends can be seen, over a decade, as data, that's to say as events for which one can prepare without really being able to affect their progress while other events (lasting between two to five years on average) may on the contrary be directly affected by our decisions (those of the leaders and/or the people).

The first part of this decade will be essentially marked, first, by the growing emergence of secular trends marking the end of Western-centrism and, secondly, by the consequences of the financial crisis and especially the reactions to it in 2009. Reactions that led to excessive state debt and, in particular, excessive debt of the mainstay of the world order in recent decades, the United States. China being the preferred vehicle for these secular trends in action and the United States being, at the same time, the country at the heart of the financial crisis and its consequences[27], we can say that it will be Sino-American relations that will determine the pace and the magnitude of the shocks that we will experience between now and the middle of the 2010-2020 period.

Similarly, the other players (new, former or reinvented[28] powers) will of course act and react in the coming years, either according to the development of the USA-China relationship and its consequences, or according to their own expectations for the world in the decades to come. It is most likely that this group that can give birth to the most fruitful initiatives and ideas to prevent the second part of the decade turning into a descent into hell for most of the planet and allow, between now and 2020, a lasting new world order to start to take shape. Given what has happened since the recognized beginning of the crisis, the USA-China duo has in fact very little chance of avoiding a sterile confrontation.

Neither the Chinese leadership, nor the U.S. elite seem to be able to do anything but defend/promote their own vested interests. Their mutual conflict and its domestic consequences for both countries will also demand all their attention, leaving them little room to think about the future of the world. That said, there is no guarantee, of course, that the contributions of the other players will be able to divert the world from the logic of a zero sum game and, therefore, conflicts between blocs such as those which will quickly establish themselves in the relationship between the USA and China. It is, moreover, for this reason that there are two accounts of the future in this book. The main difference between the two hinges on this factor: the divergence of assumed developments becoming more and more apparent during the second half of the decade. But let's not anticipate (for once) the end of the book. Let's first look at the likely developments for the main geopolitical players for the 2010-2020 decade, as well as the general framework of their interplay, in more detail.

These likely developments will be a chain of events that will lead to the disintegration of the current international system, particularly through the collapse or paralysis of the major international institutions and the strategic links of the

---

[27] This may seem surprising but I don't think that the United States would be a central player in the currently emerging secular trends. In the end they will only have been, at a global level, a substitute for European power for the time that it took the latter to complete it's painful metamorphosis from "European powers" to " the European power" during the twentieth century. It really is Europeans, as the EU, who make up one of the new potential powers of the twenty-first century, alongside China, India and Russia, not least because it was an entity that didn't exist in the world order until the 1990s. It took the fall of the Berlin Wall for the European community project to leave its experimental cocoon. We will come back to this later in the book.

[28] We can put Russia, China, India ... and the EU in this latter category. In another guise, these powers were already major historical players. While Brazil or South Africa, for example, are actually new players. Today the United States is undeniably a former power.

global monetary and financial system, and the beginning of a process of structural rebuilding of the major global players like the United States, the EU, Russia, Asia and Latin America, fluctuating between the beginning of disruption for some and the continuation of reorganization for others.

The rapid disintegration of the whole of
the current international system

This process is already underway. The failure of the Copenhagen summit on global warming in late 2009 has brought to light several features of this rapid disintegration of the current international system: the ineffective UN approach, the lack of a common Western position on the splitting of funds between Americans and Europeans, the ability to block the BRIC countries and China in particular, obsolescence of the Anglo-American marketing approach mixing « politics of fear » and « tabloid » communication, indifference to public opinion in the face of the economic and social consequences of the crisis and the loss of credibility of public institutions and the media[29].

The UN

The UN is totally overwhelmed by the current crisis. Neither the Security Council nor the various special agencies seem able to have the slightest ability to influence the unfolding events and even less on applying solutions. The absence of the United Nations on all key issues related to current geopolitics (Korea, Iran, Middle East, etc.) attests to its rapid obliteration. Moreover, the alarmist attitude of the WHO over Swine Fever has only contributed to the growing doubts of public opinion on even the credibility of the analyses published by these international agencies.

The WTO

The WTO, as we have said already, only has authority to the extent that its most influential members agree to apply its rules and decisions. At present the growing trend, behind the official rhetoric, is totally the opposite. The United States, China, the EU (at least certain member states like France or the United Kingdom) seem reluctant to do anything but let the "every man for himself" concept take hold in world trade. This is the same world trade which is in freefall and whose weakening, of course, negatively affects the WTO's ability to influence. This

---

[29] The simultaneous fiasco of the so-called terrible Swine Fever epidemic only contributes to this growing conviction of a use of collective fear to advance hidden financial, political or security agendas.

supreme creation of the period of accelerated globalization that we have experienced over the last twenty years is at an impasse. The Doha Round, its main current project, will not reach a successful conclusion whatever anyone may say officially. Its collapse only steadily gets worse each year, due to lack of leadership to bring it to fruition and because the key players are now turning to the rationale of regional integration and/or trading blocs. Incidentally, this is the only way out for the WTO in the coming decade, that is to say to try and change the functioning of an institution based on States to one based on the major regional business entities to prevent these regional free trade areas turning themselves into trading blocs in direct conflict, which these blocs will surely not fail to do without an appropriate regulatory framework at global level.

The OECD

The OECD, which basically has never been anything other than a kind of institutional think tank to promote the prevailing Western agenda is absolutely not equipped to be anything other than a muzzy sounding board for suggestions and is totally devoid of mechanisms and human resources to act on a global crisis and even less on the reorganization of global governance that it implies. To do this, it needs, in effect, strong political legitimacy, huge financial resources and particularly bold leaders, all of which are the antithesis of the respectable Château de la Muette[30].

The IMF

The IMF isn't able to have a significant impact on the crisis either. At best, it can still play the role of "broom wagon" and provide emergency support to states on the verge of bankruptcy (it is, moreover, the sole purpose for the capital increase decided by the G20, ironically by over-indebted Western states). However the increasing number of states affected as well as the size of their respective economies will pose a problem of capacity. Finally, the IMF remains essentially the financial arm of the United States and its Western allies, endowed with a decision-making structure that will not match the financial power relationships of our planet in the coming decade any more. The majority of the countries having the largest global financial reserves are marginalized there. Suffice to say they will not offer any "gift" to the IMF to see their money used without being able to actually influence its use. We can see here to what extent action should have been taken, at least ten years ago, to reform the IMF and to adapt its decision-making structure to the world of the early twenty-first century instead of leaving it bogged-down in the post-Second World War world.

---

[30] The Paris headquarters of the OECD

Moreover, it is also very indicative of the current international blockade that IMF reform, giving the BRIC countries a place suited to their new economic status, has still not been implemented. Don't give anything away unless events oblige you to seems to be the watchword of the Americans and Europeans. It's hardly surprising coming from Washington, even if it is a short-sighted attitude. For the Europeans, it is absurd. Not being the masters of the present game, they have everything to gain by actively participating in changing the rules. But in this case, instead of proposing bold reforms (reducing the number of their votes, grouping them under a common European banner and, in the same breath, demanding a similar decrease in the U.S. vote), they are on the defensive and appear to be those responsible for the lack of significant change, which is really the last straw since the first of these increasingly striking IMF distortions is the oversized influence that the United States has there.

They would also have to impose a rapid pace of change. The new voting arrangements must become fully operational between now and 2013/2014 at the latest to enable the IMF to play a role as a gyroscope, a stabilizer of the global economic and financial system of the second half of the decade. Otherwise, far from stabilizing anything, it will become another bone of contention, then clashes, between the different global players to ultimately cease having any importance. Indeed, if the political will is there, it is this institution that can give birth to the future benchmark global reserve currency without much difficulty that will enable a decisive exit from the Dollar era without passing through a state of « widespread chaos ».

The G7 and G20

The G7 (or G8) has never been anything other than an elitist club gathering round the United States and major Western economies to give the appearance of vague collegiate management of the world. Barack Obama, moreover, already signed its death warrant in 2009, reflecting the end of twenty years of Western hegemony on the planet.

Coming to the G20, the last-born of the series' merit is to combine at last the emerging powers of the twenty-first century (China, India, Brazil, etc.) with the old powers of the twentieth century. For the time being it's its only merit because its first summits have in fact produced nothing tangible on basic problems such as replacing the U.S. Dollar as the international benchmark currency. Our Western leaders, Nicolas Sarkozy and Gordon Brown in the lead, have entertained the gallery with their thundering declarations on tax havens and bankers' bonuses. The most important tax havens (around the City, like the Channel Islands, and Wall Street, such as Delaware) are not affected, as they sign "transparency" agreements between themselves to get off the black or grey list. Bankers' bonuses have already been bypassed by a raft of practices which include deserving traders being paid for providing consulting services.

The major weakness of the present G20 is that it is fundamentally dominated by leaders from the world that is in the course of collapsing under our noses. Nearly two-thirds of them belong to the Western bloc, or are leaders who depend on it to stay in power. This is not really conducive to questioning the very foundations of this crisis that affects the functioning of the Western model of these recent decades. The EU, or rather the Eurozone, would be the only one able to tilt the balance of power between the "world before" and "the world after" but for the moment, as its leaders are totally subservient to Washington, it blindly follows the United States and prevents any fundamental questioning within the G20.

However, there is a simple option enabling the Europeans to exit global governance from the impasse in which it finds itself at the beginning of this decade, namely to actively participate in one of the upcoming BRIC summits of which the first was held in June 2009 in Yekaterinburg, Russia. The Western press has been remarkably discreet over an event decisive on the global geopolitical landscape however, not so much for the decisions taken because there were none, but due to the fact that it managed to take place despite fierce opposition from Washington who were not even able to send an observer. The loss of power over a group is measured, in effect, by the inability of the leader to prevent the other members meeting to discuss matters that it is not supportive of.

No one is in any doubt that if these four countries met, it wasn't to help the U.S. maintain its global influence, or the Dollar to extend its global rule. In any event, the mere proposal from the EU, the Eurozone or even the Franco-German duo, to participate in one of the BRIC summits between now and 2014 would be such an indicator of the shift in world order that it would immediately become a factor for change in itself, a messenger of a new direction in world affairs. And it really is direction that is needed by the world when all the usual landmarks disappear. This act in itself is simple, but it can only be decided by skilled leaders[31] with an historic vision of their responsibilities. Suffice to say that we are unlikely to see that happen with the current European leaders.

---

[31] Because there are many pitfalls, especially in the EU where the United Kingdom will do everything to ensure this initiative comes to nothing or is diluted in a "Western", "Transatlantic" context which would take away any value-added to help transform global governance. Quite apart from the fact that it would, above all, culminate in making European participation in a BRIC summit impossible.

The downfall of the strategic ties of the world financial, economic, monetary and strategic system

The system currently collapsing is based mainly on the power of a few strategic ties carefully controlled by the first ranking dominant powers including the United States of course. These ties allow the control of the main flows and limits of the system, financial flows and currency exchange rates in particular. But the global systemic crisis is bringing about the downfall of these strategic ties of Wall Street, the City of London or the financial center of Tokyo, as well as a number of secondary centers such as Hong Kong, Singapore or Dubai.

Bankers and executives of financial institutions are being laid off everywhere in the tens of thousands. Banks are seeing their balance sheets shrink visibly or, out of the public eye, fill with ghost-assets which will never be worth the price attributed to them in the balance sheets. The credibility of experts and analysts who serve this small world stretches dangerously towards zero, as the case of the rating agencies shows[32]. The European Union and China soon probably will be compelled to establish their own credit rating agencies in order to avoid being deceived as they have been in the current crisis.

By 2014, it will probably be a done deed, ending a U.S.-British hegemony of over two centuries on the valuation of international financial assets, a much greater source of power than that of the gunboat or predator drone because of the ability to ruin or, on the contrary, enrich companies and States by a single wave of the magic wand. Now, who loses control of the valuation process, loses the ability to hide its weaknesses, its faults and its failures. Diversification of rating sources will, therefore, cause a major upheaval of the current system. To take one example, how can any credence be given to rating agencies that are quick to lower the rating of countries like Spain or Greece because of the pressures weighing on their solvency due to the crisis while the United Kingdom and the United States which are sinking in debt and seeing their economies devastated are not subject to any change in theirs[33]. The emergence of non-US rating agencies will dramatically put the clocks right and the ratings with it[34].

---

[32] Thus the three main rating agencies, Moody's, Fitch and Standard & Poor's, are all American and even receive several hundreds of millions of dollars from the United States government as part of its plan to buy toxic financial assets. So one can imagine their "independence" when it is a matter of "rating" the latter.

[33] Another telling example: California, the richest and most populous American state, has been plunged into such a financial crisis that since the beginning of February 2009 state employees must stop working one day a week due to a lack of funds to pay them, Californian state creditors have been paid in IOUs (due to a lack of sufficient dollars) and public services are being heavily cut (teacher layoffs, cuts in additional administrative staff, prison closings, police stations, fire stations, etc.). Have the rating agencies drawn any conclusions for the credibility of the United States? Not at all! But one can easily imagine their reaction if

Regarding the global monetary system, we find ourselves in a somewhat similar situation, nearly 70% of forex trades are conducted in three financial centres, namely London, New York and Tokyo. All three belong, de facto, to the dollar zone and depend heavily on Washington, which ensures that their interpretation of world events and developments are basically similar. The current collapse of the British economy and its financial centre threatens London's dominant role. At the same time, while eight of the ten largest banks in international currency markets were American or British in May 2008, it is remarkable that some have already disappeared from the landscape, such as Lehman Brothers, or are almost bankrupt (nationalized) as is the case of Royal Bank of Scotland or Citibank.

Here again, we see how quickly this strategic link of the global financial system is in the process of coming apart before our very eyes, contributing to an accelerated breakdown of the entire international system of recent decades between now and the middle of the 2010-2020 decade. Asia, Latin America and Euroland will, in every instance, be the winners of this development. If Wall Street is assured of keeping its position as a financial hub for North America, it will certainly be more as a regional than global centre. The end of Dollar supremacy will have an irreversible effect. For the City the outlook is very much darker. The United Kingdom has injected even more money than Washington to prevent the British financial centre's collapse.

The extent of the latter's weakness can now be seen at all levels, not least in its inability to prevent the French from taking the post of Internal Market Commissioner, whose duties include reforming the control of European financial markets. And, de facto, despite the bluster from Downing Street, the new European financial regulations really place the City under the supervision of the European community thus ending London finance's three centuries of independent power. In a certain sense, it's a simple catching up of history. If the imperial transfer of power had not taken place between two powers of the same language facing each other from each side of a small ocean (« the pond », to the Americans and English), London would have long since lost its status as the second world financial center. It is highly unlikely, with the rise in Chinese power, that history will show Wall Street as much courtesy.

The final strategic tie to unravel is, of course, the almost exclusive monopoly of the Anglo-Saxon press on economic and financial issues. For decades, and with a strengthening of the trend since the fall of the Berlin Wall, the world follows world

---

Germany (the richest and most populous state of the EU) announced such a decision: these same agencies would have deduced that the entire Eurozone faced imminent bankruptcy!

[34] For the record, the Friday preceding Lehman Brothers' bankruptcy, those agencies continued to give AAA ratings to a number of the bank's financial products. The following Monday those same products were worth nothing. The ratings of these three agencies express nothing other than the interests of the powers that control them. Those who use it to assess their investment strategy should, therefore, be on the highest alert over nasty surprises to come.

economic and financial news through the American or British media. Either the latter serves as unquestioned benchmarks of the national media that cover these topics or these same national media settle for a direct translation of the articles they publish. In France in particular, this trend has become widespread since the mid 2000s. The lack of an economic and financial education of most of the French journalists has encouraged this development which has resulted in France, as elsewhere, without the public being told, in the imposition of a sole view of financial and economic world affairs[35]. It is easy to imagine the importance of such a tool when the "king becomes totally naked". It lets one continue to believe that he is smartly dressed and serves to prevent public opinion from discovering the real alternatives available to their country or region in the years to come.

One reason for the success of the Global Europe Anticipation Bulletin (GEAB)[36], whose publications are now followed by more than ten million readers every month in more than 70 languages and 120 countries, holds good as both a reaction against this situation of an information monopoly about the true state of the global economy and finance and the media in question's undeniable loss of credibility of which the crisis has illustrated their docility and willingness to be nothing more than propaganda tools. Beyond the GEAB's telling example, we are witnessing, via the Internet in particular, a proliferation of sites and blogs that allows one to form a more realistic view of the progression of the world economy and finance. From now on it's the heads of the world's major financial institutions, government officials, politicians and business leaders who turn to this information. The crisis typically turns the "mainstream" into a flow less and less "main". The official Anglo-Saxon vision of the world delivered at length by the Financial Times, New York Times, Bloomberg, The Wall Street Journal, Economist or Market Watch crumbles quickly under the onslaught of the crisis. Today, reading the Russian, Chinese, Indian, Brazilian, German, Spanish, French (if it knows how to become a true voice again) media is equally important. Tomorrow, that's to say between now and 2020 at the latest, it will become even more important. It is also that a world order changes, we no longer read the same newspapers. Ask the sales manager of Pravda in 1989, he knows something about it!

---

[35] Le Monde in France distinguishes itself by a frenzied policy of translations of English articles while a magazine like Slate-France illustrates a distinct Americanist dialogue even at the heart of the French press, consisting mainly of translated U.S. articles. As regards Libération, it has given up on major economic issues and focuses on socio-political affairs. For its part Le Figaro remains true to itself: it always favours the strongest and, therefore, at the moment faithfully mirrors the dominant debates in the Anglo-Saxon press. Paris, because in terms of national press it is only this city that counts, has become a hub of Americanism in Europe in just a few years. And the French press is a perfect salesman for this trend. Today, there are more critical and alternative views in some English or U.S. media than in the Parisian one. That's saying something!

[36] Published by LEAP since 2006. In the second issue, in February 2006, of this newsletter LEAP announced the impending crisis.

The crisis, the catalyst of the restoration of the supremacy of the real economy over the virtual economy

The reversal of the centuries old trends we are experiencing is accompanied by the collapse of a more recent "bubble", which has gradually formed since the 1970s, and that can be called "terminal imperial growth". This is, of course, the global financial sector which, in nearly forty years, has gradually brought a virtual economy to the surface with a value greater[37] than the global substantive economy. Now an historic crisis is, above all, a great contraction of time. In a few years changes take place that are usually spread over decades, or even centuries if the crisis is a major one.

So, beginning in 2008 with the series of bankruptcies of the Wall Street giants, the federal government rescue of all the others and the emergency takeovers of British banks by the United Kingdom Government, we are witnessing the downfall of the two anchorages of the "global financial bubble". If I use the term anchorage, it's to indicate that the only value this "bubble" has is that assigned to it by the two global financial centres of New York and London who are at the heart of the network of securities' issuers, listings, rating agencies, international financial media, and issuer of the global virtual economy's currency of choice, the U.S. Dollar.

Its interaction with the real economy is mainly through these two centres which play their role well as anchorage in the actuality of the global financial bubble. Other financial centers are of minor importance compared to these two giants, especially in terms of the management/creation of all the financial instruments of these recent decades that make up the bulk of the virtual economy.

And so these two centres, that of the "high class" Anglo-Saxon Empire, London, and that of the "low class" Anglo-Saxon Empire, New York, are disintegrating before our very eyes:

- London now only exists by courtesy of the direct and massive support of the British government. Without the British taxpayer's money, the City's jewels would have disappeared in 2008. They only survive thanks to the continued provision of this support which cannot last beyond the next two years because of the crisis in the country's public finances. The country's budgetary constraints have weakened the City so much that, in 2009, it wasn't either able to prevent a sharp rise in financial sector taxation now making London one of the least fiscally attractive global financial spots on

---

[37] Just as virtual as the crisis and 30 trillion USD in ghost financial assets show.

the planet[38] or block the process of European legislation which places the City under the supervision of non-British institutions for the first time in three centuries.

- New York is also on Federal Government life support. It survives thanks only to the policy of zero cost money pursued by the Federal Reserve for nearly two years and through the latter's purchase of trillions of mortgages to prevent a widespread collapse of the entire U.S. real estate market involving a major part of the U.S. financial bubble. As in the United Kingdom, 2010/2011 will mark the end of most of these policies, leading Wall Street into a new phase of weakness.

Globally, regulation of this sector progresses, paradoxically, by the development of a trend towards its fragmentation. An increasing number of countries or regions (such as the EU) are putting in place control procedures, prohibition of certain practices or rules of their own and which, de facto, are breaking the "global" nature that has characterized the financial sector and its exponential growth since the late 1980s. Its fragmentation is actually the most effective way of deflating this "bubble" as it directly affects the modus operandi that makes it possible.

Finally, the geopolitical "raison d'être" of this "bubble" has entered its terminal phase. Indeed, the global financial sphere started its runaway growth in the 1970s first, because of the U.S. decision to let the Dollar float and secondly, the need to recycle the huge financial surpluses of the oil producing countries. This first major sign that the United States was no longer able to assume the role as a cornerstone of the world order which it had been given in 1945[39] marked the outbreak of "the unstoppable rise of the virtual economy". To still keep this fiction even further from global economic reality, the United States has thus facilitated the unreserved emergence of market participants, financial instruments and products allowing the connection to be made between their stated and real power. The virtual economy rushed in to take advantage of this "niche" that turned into a bubble[40].

In a way, and vis-à-vis the Euro, for ten years Greece has done nothing different (admittedly on a small scale) to what the United States has done for forty years. Greece has hidden the real weakness of its budgetary and financial situation by

---

[38] KPMG has just completed a paper comparing the taxation of financial institutions' employees in eight financial centers worldwide (Dubai which now has all the appearance of a ghost financial center, Hong Kong, Zurich, London, New York, Geneva, Paris and Frankfurt). The result speaks for itself. In one year, London has dropped from 4th to last place for a banker with a family and to 6th place for an unmarried banker.

[39] By ending convertibility between the Dollar and gold in 1971, the United States decided to give a virtual value to their currency and economy of which this currency is the yardstick.

[40] Especially when the claim to be the central power of a single world has only increased the gap between actual and declared power.

resorting to the same banks and financial techniques as those used by Washington (or London) for several decades to hide the true state of affairs of their economies. But because of the crisis, the Euro's constraints of the forces have suddenly obliged Greece to restore conformity between the real and the virtual status of its finances and prosperity. The United States, facing a world that increasingly challenges the Dollar, is reluctantly involved in the same process, which will simultaneously mark the final implosion of the global financial bubble, consisting primarily of financial assets denominated in Dollars.

From this point of view, the acceleration of events of which the crisis is both the omen and the catalyst is contributing to burst the "bubble" of the virtual economy by weakening all the factors that have allowed it to exist and develop, and making its operators and methods increasingly dubious.

To finish on the end of the domination of the virtual economy, consider this telling picture. What politician today would still be photographed with the head of Goldman Sachs[41]? Probably none of those coming up for election in the next few years. Yet, two years ago, it was the kind of "Davos style" photo which symbolized "innovation". Such a change, so radical in less than two years, illustrates the strength of the headwinds that the virtual economy must now confront[42]. Its "high priests" become pariahs. And in losing close contact with policy makers, the operators at the heart of the global virtual economy lose control of the conditions, or even the substance, of their businesses: the control of regulations, regulators and opinion leaders which allowed them, on the one hand, to arbitrarily assign value to what was simply a virtual asset disconnected from any social or economic purpose and, on the other hand, show extraordinary returns generated by bespoke deregulation.

Mario Draghi, whose attempt to succeed Jean-Claude Trichet has now completely foundered due to his former role as head of Goldman Sachs Europe, is a good example of what the rout of the virtual economy will cause throughout the world among the elite. The financier, previously acclaimed, becomes suspect, notably allowing the comeback of the engineer. Today's students are already anticipating these changes. The now stigmatized social role of finance combined with massive cuts in jobs and wages in the sector have reduced the flow of clever people who were leaving science, engineering or other sectors of the real economy to rush into investment banks and hedge funds. A sector which loses its attractiveness in terms of human resources, which sees the power of its main

---

[41]The way in which Goldman Sachs got entangled in the Greek case perfectly illustrates the changing times. What was only "simple routine" for the virtual economy two years ago, financially engineering public debt, has become a dangerous practice firmly fixed in this political, social and economic reality to which the crisis has restored precedence, or if one prefers, the restoration of precedence causing the crisis.

[42] And the advance of the coming years are only going to strengthen these headwinds, whereupon the consequences of the crisis will become more dramatic for everyone.

centres dissolve, which can no longer control its regulatory environment and in which profitability is declining, has its future behind it. This is exactly the case of the virtual economy. Moreover isn't China, which appears to be one of the big winners in this crisis, governed by engineers while the United States, the big loser, by financiers?

2010-2020 decade, towards a knockout victory by the gold over the Dollar

All empires' major reversals of fortune have had gold as a protagonist or, to be more precise, the growing impossibility for those same empires to keep their gold reserves in an attempt to sustain their power. However, ultimately gold is only a medium/long term investment intended to preserve one's capital against the risk of the loss of value of paper currencies and financial assets and an eventual means of payment in case of a very serious monetary crisis. In both cases, the choice of investing a portion of one's assets in gold holdings matches an anticipation of events and risks in the coming years (and not in the coming weeks or months). Because of the crisis, this decade will see gold's big comeback in the international monetary system winning by a knockout over the U.S. Dollar, its great adversary of the past sixty years. Effectively, for the first time in nearly 40 years (since the end of the Dollar's convertibility into gold in 1971), the interests of global central banks and individual investors converge once again here. The guarantee of value is not at all assured by the Dollar as an international reserve currency and as long as it has no recognized global successor, gold will remain the only asset with the ability to have durable lasting value. The U.S. Federal Reserve is no longer able to continue its multi decade fight against the "barbarous relic" in order to ensure the supremacy of the U.S. currency at the core of the international monetary system.

If the market for the yellow metal seems to have been organized by the Fed and major central banks to prevent any significant appreciation in the price of gold, the fact remains that because of the global systemic crisis, the structural collapse of the United States' influence (and therefore the Fed's) and the related breakdown of the international monetary system inherited from 1971, gold is a safe investment in highly uncertain times. As a reminder, it has gained over 100% in U.S. Dollars and more than 85% in Euros since the beginning of the subprime crisis in mid-2006. But if gold's price has increased considerably since then, this is not due to market developments towards greater transparency and less U.S. Federal Reserve manipulation and its major counterparts. The three main devices used to try to prevent any return of gold to the core of the international monetary system are still in place, that's to say:

- The development of a "paper gold" market diluting the physical gold market in an sea of fictitious contracts because they are, in the main, pledges on gold that doesn't really exist (or, what amounts to the same, used several times for different contracts).

- The manipulation of the level of physical gold reserves, in particular those of the United States which has not been subjected to any independent audit for decades.

- The policy of systematic stories in the major economic and financial media aiming to stigmatize investment in gold as an archaic response, reserved for old people who only swear by gold in the same way they talk about their forgotten wars, and for gold maniacs that the precious metal make mad.

As everyone has been seeing over the last forty years and until a short time ago, this strategy has worked remarkably well even causing many countries, including the United Kingdom at the forefront[43], to get rid of their gold reserves at rock-bottom prices. Thus this anecdote is a very good illustration of the need for leaders to have either a good personal capacity to anticipate events or at least to have access to this kind of anticipation. In this case, the bill for the failure to anticipate has been at least ten billion USD.

But if the organization of the market that allowed gold to be kept at a distance from the international monetary system for forty years continued to be operational, what has really changed to make this sharp rise in the price of gold possible nevertheless?

It is the reversal of a key factor in the global order because of the growing impact of the systemic crisis and the entering into the phase of global geopolitical dislocation: the U.S. Federal Reserve no longer has the means to fight against this ancient enemy of U.S. Dollar hegemony that gold represents. This loss is, of course, a complex event with many facets:

• The Fed needs to bail out all the U.S. economic players' balance sheets in an attempt to prevent widespread bankruptcy. So it floods the U.S. economy, and consequently the world's, with liquidity to cause an escalation in value of all conceivable assets (or at least to stop their depreciation): real estate by purchasing mortgages, financial assets by stimulating stock exchanges and other specialized markets, and suddenly, that affects raw materials, energy and precious metals, including gold. The panic of U.S. monetary authorities, spread in varying degrees by other major central banks (particularly the Bank of England and the People's Bank of China), therefore contributing to this rise in the price of gold.

---

[43] Gordon Brown was the architect of this brilliant economic-financial error that has so far cost the British Treasury more than 10 billion USD. That said, the British taxpayers can console themselves by saying that if there had been ten billion more in their coffers, their government would have given it to the banks in recent months as well. And to raise their spirits, they should know that Nicolas Sarkozy, then French finance minister, orchestrated a less significant but equally ideological sale of the country's gold. No comment!

. The transformation of the Fed into a mega-bank of the U.S. economy, directly guaranteeing the survival of whole swathes of the country's economic sectors (real estate, automotive, finance, etc.) as well as the federal government itself (more than half the U.S. Treasury Bond issuance now ends up on the Fed's balance sheet) by a massive inclusion of their depreciated securities on its own balance sheet causes it to lose all credibility on two strategic fronts: its status as a central bank with almost unlimited powers of action[44] and its status as the central bank of the most powerful economy and state in the world. But without this dual status, the Fed is nothing more than a "paper tiger", to quote Mao Tse Tung[45]. For millennia, wealth and power are just what gold is meant to bring those who own it. Ironically, it is precisely by recouping all the world's gold following two world wars that the United States has been able to build its international power and that of the dollar. Clearly it's a history lesson forgotten by U.S. leaders in recent decades.

• The inability of the United States and its Western allies to continue to control global governance[46] of which the emergence of the G20 is a clear sign, coupled with the inability of this same G20 to begin defining a new international monetary system, opens a period of indefinite length during which paper currencies no longer have any landmarks ("master currency") and therefore no firm anchorage. We are, therefore, entering a new period of sharp declines in currencies relative to the price of gold as we have seen in the past.

Accordingly, central banks in most of the world and the players in charge of financial assets held for the long term (sovereign funds, pension funds, insurance, etc.[47]) and individual investors have begun to reintroduce gold in the international monetary system. There are, of course, no major political statements, or decisions announced publicly. It would be for the G20, or at least a BRIC-EU coalition, to make such statements. But truly, they are unable to do so because of the inability of European politics to assert itself as a global independent player. So, as always happens in history, the lowly and unranked[48], motivated by their well understood interests and their own interpretation of events, undertake to fundamentally alter the gold market's landscape. If one were to take a simple image to represent the evolution of the next decade, one could say that central banks around the world will progressively become buyers of gold again.

---

[44] The questions now focus on the risks of the Fed's bankruptcy and not on the limits of its power.

[45] And Beijing is directly involved in this transformation of the Fed into a sparrow-scarer. If that surely delights Beijing geopoliticians, it will nevertheless cost the country's economy and finances dearly except, notably, to rapidly and massively increase gold purchases.

[46] Of which the Fed was, for decades, the only master and commander in terms of its monetary component.

[47] Even the largest global market for financial derivative products, the Chicago Mercantile Exchange, has begun to accept gold as a means of settlement on its exchanges.

[48] Finally as it turns out, it is rather the powerful and discreet infra-state players trying to avoid any sudden developments, especially in the fall of the Dollar; and any risk of direct reprisals by the United States which can still react absent it acting.

And that will last for as long as there is no structural reform of the global monetary system, allowing the emergence of a new international reserve currency. Given the historic opportunity missed by the G20 summit in London in April 2009, it is now unlikely that such a development will occur until at least 2014, with the changes in political leadership in Europe. Otherwise, we will have to wait until the next decade. Throughout this period, investing in physical gold has a bright future ahead of it[49].

To conclude, let's look at the subject representative of the general crisis of confidence in the Fed and the U.S. Treasury on the true amount of gold owned by the United States. Divided between Fort Knox and the Federal Reserve Bank of New York, the exact quantity of yellow metal has generated lasting controversy in the United States because it has not been independently audited (by the U.S. Congress for example) for at least forty years. GATA, the "Gold Anti-Trust Action Committee" which, since 1999, gathers together players who wish to make the gold market transparent and, in particular, know the true state of the Federal Reserve's stocks of the yellow metal, has made many approaches to the U.S. Treasury and the Fed on this issue. At this point, the "independent" audit to which the U.S. authorities have referred was conducted by KPMG in 2006 without resolution notably on the issue of the nature of the audit procedures[50] or that it dealt with nothing other than a sampling of the reserves. This uncertainty over the exact amount of official U.S. reserves is also fueled by the growing suspicion that, through swap agreements or other emergency measures (and with the current crisis the Fed and U.S. Treasury have not lacked emergencies), the United States has been obliged to secretly part with an increasing share of its gold[51] reserves while accounting for this as Dollars. Those who still think that the books of our states and central banks are transparent should bear two recent events in mind: Bloomberg, despite a succession of lawsuits, still cannot get the Fed to provide it with the list of U.S. banks that have had the benefit of hundreds of billions of public funds since autumn 2008; the British discovered a some time ago in the midst of the same storm that their central bank had injected more than 60 billion pounds into two major banks in the country without any expert realizing it.

On this question of the exact amount of United States' gold reserves, one touches on highly sensitive subjects for which the lie becomes an "absolute reason

---

[49] Especially as the world's gold reserves appear to be rapidly decreasing.

[50] To follow this important discussion in detail, here are two links that summarize the controversy over the nature of the audits and identifies several sources to complete the information: Moderate Observer, 30/01/2008; Times, 28/03/2009. The Times reports, in particular, that the U.S. Treasury has confirmed to it that the independent auditors never had direct access to the reserves themselves in Fort Knox

[51] It would be interesting to see if China in particular has not received U.S. gold to prevent it embarking on a rejection of the Dollar and U.S. Treasury Bonds. Blackmail politics also exists between States.

of state"[52]. The secondary nature of a country's gold reserves in a "modern"[53] economy is an "ideological truth" of the same order as "the end of history", "the new model of unending economic growth", "U.S. real estate which can only go up in value", "the impossibility of a serious crisis", etc. all "truths" that have proved to be base lies once reality has caught up with them. In this case, this issue reminds one of the problems caused since March 2006 by the Federal Reserve stopping publication of the M3 indicator (the most representative measure of movements in U.S. money supply) which makes it increasingly difficult to assess the monetary situation of the country. The disappearance of this indicator was one of the symbolic factors that had allowed me, with the LEAP team, to announce the imminent outbreak of the global systemic crisis. It now seems that this question of the true amount of the United States' gold reserves, set against a background of gold's major return to the international monetary system, could provide the trigger for the next sharp drop in the U.S. Dollar. It is, therefore, a factor to monitor carefully in the months and years ahead.

Nuclear Proliferation 2010-2020
Towards a new treaty or in the direction of world chaos

Among these ties of the world before the crisis that either become hangman's nooses strangling the emergence of the "world after" or will be sliced like the Gordian knot thus allowing, on the contrary, a move to a new global organization, there is the crucial question of nuclear proliferation currently represented by the controversy over Iran.

The return of the Iranian nuclear issue to the front of the international stage owes nothing to chance. After a break of a year because of Wall Street's implosion in September 2008, all major geopolitical trends at work in the preceding period have resurfaced (the resumption of the U.S. Dollar' downfall is a glaring example). It is thus the Iranian nuclear crisis which comes to the forefront of global geopolitical concerns, in a context even more volatile than 12 months ago. Indeed, in the meantime, the United States has suddenly entered a period of historic weakness exemplified today by a new president whose hesitation-waltzes and

---

[52] To understand the close connection between "treasure" and "empire", it is worth studying the history of the Delian League. Delos was a Greek island where Athens deposited the treasure of the Delian league which it had created to oppose the Persians and later became its instrument of domination over Greek cities. Think about how the end of that league came about.

[53] To understand the close connection between "treasure" and "empire", it is worth studying the history of the Delian League. Delos was a Greek island where Athens deposited the treasure of the Delian league which it had created to oppose the Persians and later became its instrument of domination over Greek cities. Think about how the end of that league came about.

progressive engulfing in a multitude of domestic and international issues is leading countries to prepare themselves to force destiny, especially Iran or Israel.

Their strategy is to transform the impasses into opportunities. However, there is a way to use the Iranian nuclear crisis to both stabilize the Middle East and give the world several decades of global strategic stability. This is the conversion of the "Nuclear Nonproliferation" treaty, which has become completely obsolete, into a treaty of "Controlled Nuclear Dissemination".

In effect, Europeans, Russians and Chinese have to launch a radical reform of the Nuclear Non-Proliferation Treaty (NPT) and all the mechanisms and machinery which hold it together. It must be adapted to the reality of the twenty-first century and based on the concept of "Controlled Nuclear Dissemination, CND". Scientific advances and lower costs today facilitate increasing access to nuclear technology. It follows that it is difficult to distinguish between the mechanisms and fields of civil and military nuclear power (as the risks of "dirty bombs" show).

This implies that today we can now count nearly forty recognized or concealed nuclear and quasi-nuclear powers which can acquire nuclear weapons very quickly (compared to five at the time the NPT was signed). Moreover, in a world that knows that the nuclear deterrent can, in some cases, guarantee peace (Cold War), the major concern now is the possession of nuclear weapons by infra-state organizations (nuclear terrorism). In short, the NPT doesn't work anymore and the attempts of the Western nuclear club to control developments have been in vain for at least two decades.

The Iran/USA/Israel crisis must thus be treated as a key moment of the general crisis in the current international system and particularly the obsolescence of the nuclear non-proliferation policy practiced since 1945. It marks the end of the order established after 1945. This crisis is a direct confrontation between two, now outdated, philosophies: that of the Iranian leaders who ignore collective global interests to focus on their own short-term national interests and that of U.S. and Israeli leaders who identify their own interests with those of the rest of world.

The nuclear non-proliferation policy inherited from the aftermath the Second World War is in crisis illustrated by: the growing number of nuclear powers that haven't signed the Non-Proliferation Treaty, the current crisis with Iran, a country that has signed the treaty however, the chase by the United States especially in the development of new types of nuclear weapons like "mini bombs", the non-sanctioned role of Pakistan in active proliferation and the recent agreement between the USA and India which completely ignores the Treaty. Given this context, and because of the very serious consequences of a potential conflict, the Iran/USA/Israel crisis cannot be treated as a special case. It must be managed by giving it a long term vision, based on new methods adapted to the realities of the twenty-first century.

But before discussing the concept of controlled dissemination in more detail, let's briefly return to Iran's situation. Because, to solve a problem, is it still necessary to set out precise terms, outside of all ideology or a priori. So, let's imagine the United States without nuclear weapons surrounded by Mexico and Canada who possess them, or even France surrounded by countries holding nuclear weapons (and which haven't signed any international treaty on nuclear power) without having them itself. How long would it take for Washington or Paris to refuse a nuclear non-proliferation treaty[54] and to set off building a nuclear arsenal at top speed?

Certainly less time than it takes to conjure up such a scenario! And Paris, like Washington, would invoke national security requirements to justify and free itself from any treaty. This is exactly the context of the Iranian crisis. Tehran is surrounded by nuclear powers (Russia, Israel, Pakistan and possibly Saudi Arabia) and, the icing on the cake over the last three years, some of its closest neighbors, like Iraq, Afghanistan or Kuwait have been converted into U.S. military bases.

So, even without an fundamentalist at its head, like the current President Mahmoud Ahmadinejad, it is not surprising to see Iran try by any means, and as quickly as possible, to equip itself with nuclear weapons. The opposite would have been surprising, especially taking into account the tremendous lesson in realpolitik given by the Bush administration that has shown the world that a dictator with nuclear weapons (North Korea) was untouchable while a dictator without (and with oil like Iraq) was a prime target.

The lesson was heard, one of the worst that could have fed international thought in recent decades, because it removed any element other than that which the simple relationship of brute force brought. It is thus certain that Iran will move at lightning speed towards the mastery of nuclear weapons to "protect" its territory, as did France, under De Gaulle's impetus, and Israel in the 60s[55].

Let's be clear. This is now an inevitable development, except for destroying Iran. The Bush administration and all the proponents of the war in Iraq, by their intellectual poverty and greed for oil, have accelerated this process. And it certainly isn't today, with the United States and the West appearing increasingly weak and divided (financial economic and social crisis, Afghanistan, etc.), that Iran will change its mind.

Just as Israel equipped itself with nuclear weapons to ensure its survival and strengthen its position in the region, Iran seeks to own nuclear weapons. Tel Aviv and Tehran are two sides of the same coin as regards nuclear armaments. Thus, apart from UN posturing and a very limited embargo, Washington, Paris, London

---

[54] While Iran hasn't rejected the treaty it signed at all, unlike Israel, Pakistan and India.

[55] The two countries also cooperated in the development of the Israeli bomb.

and Berlin will no nothing. It's too late. The Russians and Chinese now have other interests and a much greater influence. We cannot rewrite history[56].

On the other hand, one can choose to collectively exit a dead end by taking a new path: in this case, turning the page of a policy of "nuclear non-proliferation", now outdated and ineffective, to embark on the path of a policy of "controlled nuclear dissemination" which, particularly, will allow the guarantee of Iran's security, like its neighbors, with a controlled practice of regional deterrence.

The new NPT, the CND treaty, must also take a leaf out of developments achieved in the international order since the 60s, with three promising lines of thought:

- Address civilian and military nuclear development together: access to the Nuclear Club should no longer have the aim of preventing the development of nuclear weapons by giving permission to develop civilian nuclear power, but really to convince of the uselessness of nuclear weapons' development or restrict it to incorporate it as a balanced regional or global deterrent should the opposite occur.

- Define the rules of access to the « Nuclear Club », based not on an arbitrary approach of the powers already members of the Club, but on a transparent process of membership, including clear and internationally recognized rules and multilateral control of their observance once a member of the club. Examples of the process of accession to the European Union or the World Trade Organization can usefully serve as a model for the definition of a "politico-nuclear acceptance" which should define the conditions of access to the whole of nuclear technology. Amongst other things, it should include the need for democratic developments in internal politics (free elections, political control of the military), the signing of regional security agreements linked if possible to regional economic and trade cooperation agreements.

- Rethink a number of the NPT's fundamental assumptions now overtaken by history. The new dimension of possession of nuclear weapons by non-state entities must be integrated to ban this likelihood and define the strictest possible sanctions. At the same time, we must abandon the axiom claiming that nuclear weapons in themselves, and in every situation, are destabilizing. Indeed, European history of the second half of the twentieth century has proved that this assertion was false. Balanced deterrence can also bring peace when it is impossible to create nuclear-free zones (which will

---

[56] Barack Obama's elegant hollow words on the abolition of nuclear weapons once again illustrates the extent to which this President is completely out of touch with geopolitical realities (unless this is a cheap way of getting the Nobel Peace Prize) an important one of which is that, thanks to nuclear weapons, the current global crisis has not turned into a series of open conflicts (as had been the case during the American-Soviet crisis). And, sadly, this state of mind distances the United States from making a realistic contribution to the reform of the NPT.

nevertheless remain the primary objective of any policy aimed at controlling nuclear risks).

As can be seen behind the Iranian crisis a major step completely changing the world is emerging, triggered after the fall of the Berlin Wall. We are still in the process of leaving the world created after 1945 behind, and the global systemic crisis is accelerating this trend. To find the path of the "world after", we have the choice between Achilles' blind arrogance and Ulysses' sharp intellect, between a non-proliferation which is an increasingly virtual activity of an illegitimate power based on prejudice and a controlled dissemination that aims to coherently integrate reality to apply rules acceptable to everyone involved.

Trying to avoid the worst consequences of the current global geopolitical dislocation is also to be bold in the nuclear field. The paradox, but it is only apparent, is that this is certainly the best way to guarantee Israel's and the whole of the Middle East's security. The nuclear deterrent is a balancing factor widely tested in the twentieth century, which prevented conflicts which, without the threat of these weapons, would undoubtedly have occurred.

Strategic dislocation of the big global players

Global geopolitical dislocation will, of course, also directly affect the major global players like the United States, China, Russia, Latin America and the EU for example. The same destructive forces will be brought to bear on these extensive political entities. In fact, the more the political entity is important in size and population, the more it rests on the « Dollar/Debts » base characteristic of the current system and the more it is centralized, the more it will prove sensitive to the tremendous pressures generated by the global systemic crisis.

If the second factor is particularly obvious (based on the Dollar/Debt base), the first is explained by the presence of a greater diversity of economic, social and financial circumstances between regions and/or social groups in the major political entities than in small countries. It is, then, the question of socio-economic cohesion in the face of the consequences of the crisis.

Lastly, the third factor, the centralization of power and, therefore, the method of analyzing the crisis and implementing responses to it matches the crucial issue of relevance of the policies that have been put in place. The crisis takes many forms and in the major political entities, the challenge of the best way to navigate the crisis might just be to place oneself in the position of fine tuning responses depending on the situation. The "same size fits all" is probably not the most effective way to address this crisis within the major political entities. This factor combines with the prevailing trend to regional integration which can sometimes lead to a country restructuring in order to make them compatible with regional integration.

The United States facing the historic "perfect storm"

For the United States the process of strategic dislocation from 2010 has become so topical that it is one of the four themes of a report presented to the Pentagon in December 2008 by Nathan P. Freier of the Strategic Studies Institute of the United States' Army War College[57]. In it he describes the risk of dismemberment of the United States' territory and its borders under the impact of the crisis[58]. Indeed, if one considers the three key factors mentioned above, the United States is at the heart of a "perfect storm"[59] in this regard:

- Of the four political entities considered it is that which relies entirely on the « Dollar/Debts » base. It is even that which has fueled their power and wealth in these recent decades. And today the whole of their financial system has become insolvent whilst Dollar creation spirals out of control[60].

- The socio-economic fabric of the country is far more diverse than an idealized vision of a uniform America from East to West would have us believe. Socio-ethnic tensions are huge with, henceforth, a strong Hispanic element linked to drug traffickers that plague the country's southern border. The different regions' economic interests increasingly diverge in the face of the crisis: for example, California's near-bankruptcy problems are not the same at all as those of states where the auto industry is collapsing and they are different again from Florida's. Texas does not have the same problems as New York, and so on. And the richest states are unwilling to pay for the poorest, a classic event leading to secession.

- Finally, the quasi-monopoly of Washington and the Federal state in the response to the crisis requires the use of highly centralized plans, standardized and therefore unable to take the widely varying situations from one State to another into account. This simple fact already guarantees that the measures already implemented will not be very effective, as we have seen elsewhere for more than a year.

---

[57] Source: Strategic Studies Institute, 04/11/2008

[58] The border with Mexico is becoming a battleground for drugs trafficking. Source: Armed Forces Journal, 01/2009; Spacewar, 05/06/2008

[59] Orage parfait

[60] There are now over 1,000 U.S. banks that will go bankrupt between now and 2014. Source: MarketWatch, 09/02/2009

At this stage it seems useful to recall that in choosing to be inspired by Abraham Lincoln, the new U.S. President has taken a significant historical risk because Lincoln was not only the end of slavery, but also the Civil War and the Greenback, the currency created by the Government without the backing of gold or silver[61], intended to finance the Civil War effort and which subsequently ignited very high inflation in the United States. Barack Obama should be wary of history which has a tendency to be very ironic.

The fact is that since the end of the nineteenth century, the disparities between States and social groups of the country were basically buried under a flood of Dollars and, more recently, debt to anesthetize against the risk of serious conflicts between States, or between some States and Washington. Besides, the success of this policy means that today few Americans, and virtually none of their political elite, have realized that their vast country is far from being a "gift of God", but is a creation of military conquest and the influx of wealth. All it needs is for the latter to just be lacking for the most conflicting aspects to quickly come to the forefront.

It is also significant that many States (Vermont, Texas, Hawaii, Alaska, Montana, Arizona, and Tennessee), begin to legislate in different directions to prevent Washington from depriving them of a particular prerogative (firearms control, health service, only using the Dollar for commercial transactions, etc.). When it's not simply local authorities (counties) that threaten to no longer pay over collected taxes in the face of the deficiencies of bankrupt federal States like California especially.

The Obama administration's recovery plan, amounting to 780 billion USD for 2009/2010, is of no earthly use. Too little, too fragmented, and especially it does not take scope of the crisis into account. Unemployment continues to rise despite all kinds of statistical chicanery. 2010 will see the actual unemployment rate affecting 20% of the workforce and the economy (from banks to the automotive or defense industries) will only survive by being drip-fed with public money.

This plan has, on the other hand, demonstrated the strong partisan divide that still prevails in Washington[62], while a single power, the military machine, now seems to float above the democratic process. It is indeed more surprising to see that, from the Minister of Defence to the leading generals, not one leader of the

---

[61] The "conventional" Dollar has continued to be issued by the United States Central Bank.

[62] And the recent Democrats' election failure to replace Ted Kennedy in the Senate will further strengthen the general stasis in Washington because of this violent partisan opposition. In addition to the expression of popular resentment against the U.S. elite leaders, this result marks the effective end of the "Obama dream". Beyond the message of hope in terms of racial integration in the United States, Barack Obama is only a "rep" much more presentable to the same powers than those who ran the Bush presidency, namely Wall Street and the military-industrial complex against whose influence President Dwight D. Eisenhower had tried in vain to warn the American people in his farewell speech. This is also a great example of missed anticipation. He had anticipated the problem, but his warning was not enough to prevent it. This illustrates how anticipation must produce action and not just rhetoric and that it must be undertaken before the problem becomes obvious.

U.S. defense apparatus has changed whilst one of the motives of Barack Obama's voters was precisely to completely overturn the military rationale of the Bush years. The policy being followed in Afghanistan illustrates the complete control of the military over Washington's political power. Politicians change but the military and their political leaders stay.

This may be a sign that a number of U.S. officials have a certain awareness that soon the army will be the final guarantor of the country's territorial integrity... and this is nothing other than Nathan P. Freier's thesis suggests. Faced with politicians' inability to picture a scenario of the country's disintegration, it is necessary that the military began to prepare. There is no need to expound on the consequences of such a development that will mark the entire Western strategic system's collapse, which today wholly revolves around United States' military power. Paradoxically, a disintegration of the United States federation, which would inevitably cause a corresponding similar break-up in Canada and Mexico, risks being an unavoidable path to shape North America to the twenty-first century.

If the latter must be characterized by European-style regional integration as we have seen gradually asserting itself in Latin America, Asia and Africa, then North America today, directly inherited from the nineteenth century, is undoubtedly the continent least well adapted to the coming decades. The United States' huge disparity in economic, demographic and geopolitical clout over its neighbours, Mexico and Canada, makes such a regional integration impossible as one can see, incidentally, in the current predicament posed by NAFTA.

And if the nation-state was the rising force that relentlessly shaped the organization of the continents between the seventeenth and nineteenth centuries, gradually destroying any other form of sovereign political body, it seems that freely agreed regional integration is the new historic format rapidly emerging all over the world. If this theory is confirmed, during the 2010 decade, North America will be criss-crossed by a growing number of fault lines that will then enable it to reconstitute itself in a form more suited to the world after the crisis.

Finally, 2009 marked a profound change in U.S. citizens' mental landscape that will lead to accelerating domestic political turmoil. Indeed, for the first time, a vast majority of Americans have realized that the country was ruled by a clique of bankers and businessmen. What, until now, was a discussion limited to the fringes of the extreme left or right of the states' political landscape has become predominant. Even the mainstream media publicly question the manifest collusion between the U.S. administration (including Barack Obama's which was supposed to embody the break vis-à-vis the Bush years on this subject) and Wall Street.

The Internet has already resolved the matter because the country's dominance by Wall Street bankers is no longer even a topic of debate. What is discussed is how to end this situation. Even the United States Congress, via proposals for the pure and simple abolition or political control of the U.S. Federal Reserve, speaks openly about these issues without elected representatives being accused of being communists. Only the European media and political leaders continue to believe that discussing these aspects of United States power is an act of blatant anti-Americanism.

The case of Congressman Ron Paul of Texas also stands out. Ultra-marginal even three years ago, he has now become a public figure who is listened to and recognized. Bearer of a "Confederate" vision of the country's future, combining isolationism, rejection of Federal power, return to the gold standard and a very "white" vision of America, his meteoric rise on the U.S. political landscape is an indication of the rapidly growing unease of a majority of people over the "American model" as much for its socio-economic as political aspect. This growing questioning will generate the principal domestic disturbances of the decade because essentially nothing has prepared the U.S. people for this type of test.

The Constitution is considered to be sacred text, its eternal validity unquestioned. And belief in the morality of a system based on the opportunity for everyone to get rich has removed any calling into question of the country's elite for several decades. The crisis is causing these two cornerstones to give way. To survive the emergency of the September 2008 shock, Wall Street was unable to take the customary precautions and thus had to act in broad daylight, or almost. And, therefore, the Americans have found, aghast in the main, that the bankers have directly picked their pockets to bail themselves out and that their government is at their beck and call[63].

The 2010-2020 decade will resonate with this sudden awareness, reinforced by the discovery from 2010 that this policy, far from helping the United States to exit the crisis more quickly will only, once again, plunge an even greater number of Americans even deeper into it. The country's ruling class will painfully learn a fundamental lesson that history teaches. Manipulation of the people only works if it remains hidden. Once exposed, it can only trigger rebellion or revolution. We celebrated, not long ago, the twentieth anniversary of the fall of Ceausescu, of which the trigger was a public meeting where the crowd began to whistle. One can easily imagine an identical situation in 2011/2012 for Ben Bernanke, head of the Federal Reserve (true holder of ultimate power in the United States and accountable to no one).

To prepare for the event, he can ask Tim Geithner's advice, U.S. Treasury Secretary, who had to face the jeers of Chinese students in Beijing in autumn 2008, when he stated that Chinese assets were secure by being invested in U.S. Treasury Bonds. When an imperial power is ridiculed abroad, it's not very far from the point of being rejected domestically.

---

[63] A similar event took place in France in 2009 even though it wasn't as intense as the American situation because of the less violent shock the country suffered.

It has taken one hundred years for this remark of Henry Ford, following the creation of the United States Federal Reserve in 1913, to become reality: "It is fortunate that the people do not understand how our banking and monetary system functions because otherwise there would be a revolution the next day". The realization happened at the turn of the decade, if Ford was right, the aftermath will happen very quickly in the first half of the decade.

The European Union in the face of its destiny as a future-maker
Between global switchman or National-Europeanism

If the U.S. represents the "unthinkable strategic break up", the European Union, particularly the Eurozone, is the "carefully thought out strategic break up". A day doesn't go by without the British or U.S. media, learnt by heart by the French media ranging from militant Americanism to aggressive anti-Europeanism[64], delivering its prognosis on the imminent collapse of the EU and/or Euro from the blows of the crisis.

Anything goes. "Shock" expressions like the designation "Club Med" for the Eurozone's Mediterranean countries. The scoops that aren't, on the colossal exposure of European banks at risk of default from Central and Eastern European countries[65]. The debt downgrades of Eurozone countries such as Greece and Spain meant to jeopardize the Eurozone, whilst these countries represent a much smaller share of the U.S. economy than the American States in near bankruptcy such as California, Florida or Michigan. And, of course, the relentless hounding of any politician, any European "expert" who would bring grist to their mill. With 27 countries and 500 million citizens, it is fairly easy to find any opinion, for or against.

---

[64] Both trends are, outwardly, opposed because one advocates the dissolution of France in the "West" (the "great struggle" in the future would be between the West and the forces of evil coming from other civilizations, being exactly what Hitler, Pétain, Franco and Mussolini thought!) while the other feeds on the idea of a "Great Nation" (France has a separate destiny and the world awaits its message: of De Gaulle performing again in the cafes of Saint Germain des Prés). However, in truth it meets up with their provincialism and outdated nature.

Provincialism because only a narrow mindset can imagine that one can only exist by submitting to the powerful of the day or, on the contrary, pretending to be able to do everything alone. Outdated because these two ideas have already had their day. America, all powerful at the West's heart is dying before our eyes. As for France, the world awaits the message that it is only a small player against China and India. Nicolas Sarkozy embodies these two "policies" perfectly, that are leading the French to become history if they do not quickly end it.

[65] The London Telegraph has, moreover, made a speciality of this topic. It's a shame because it's a newspaper that is often very incisive and well informed on economic and financial matters. Besides, we often cite it as a source. But for years, long before the crisis, it was becoming noticeable that some of its economics journalists are pathological "Eurosceptics", not hesitating to twist the information to serve their argument. The fall in the pound and the U.S. depression only seems to have re-kindled their ardour, leading them to say anything for some time now.

But let's take the time to address the substance of the statement that European banks are more exposed than U.S. banks to hundreds of billions of toxic assets particularly from Eastern Europe. This assertion is in fact emblematic of a thought process that still does not understand the nature of the current crisis. Because even if this were true in terms of exposure (except, that it is far from being proved, for the Austrian banks), we must realize that today, on our planet, there is nothing more toxic than a working U.S. financier[66]. Taking real estate as an example (which is mainly the case in Eastern Europe), the situation is very clear:

- In Central and Eastern Europe, after fifty years of communist non-investment, there is a huge need for real estate (as much for housing as commercial premises). So, even though prices have been excessive in recent years, property has a real value and will easily find buyers at a reasonable discount. Therefore, banks with these properties are holding assets that have substantial value.

- In the United States, the real estate frenzy of recent years has led to the building of millions of simply unnecessary[67] homes and business premises, often built in a hurry and of poor quality. With one home in nine now empty, U.S. banks hold assets which are, de facto, worth nothing anymore and that, as time passes, will inevitably deteriorate.

It's hard for journalists from the City or Wall Street to grasp, but a house in Romania or Hungary is an asset that actually has a much greater value than a house in San Diego, Detroit or Miami (or an apartment in the 800 meters high Burj Dubai tower). With this small reminder out of the way, we can return to the issue of strategic dislocation of the EU or the Eurozone.

It is certain that this crisis is in the process of creating a two-speed Europe, and certainly one with two types of institutions, the Eurozone on one side and the other members of the EU on the other. However, this event is nothing more than the latest version of the historical process of European integration. For nearly 60 years the Europeans have been progressing like that: first a core of trailblazing countries, then the other countries that join them.

Another feature of the EU which paradoxically makes it less susceptible to forces that could take it apart, is precisely that everyone fears this possibility and therefore everyone discusses it, bringing forth a bunch of possible solutions, unthinkable today but perhaps growing in evidence tomorrow[68]. There again, Europeans are used to the fact.

---

[66] Except perhaps a working British or Dubain financier

[67] This is the ghost mall syndrome that spreads across the country as shops close.

[68] Thus, in the case of a risk of default by Ireland or Greece, it is more than likely that the emergency will require Germany, France and some other countries to come to the rescue of the country concerned. It is an

Finally, the Eurozone countries have solvent citizens which therefore offers the possibility for countries to significantly increase the tax burden if necessary (which will be the case between 2010-2014). This is another fundamental difference compared to the United States where the majority of the population is in debt and in fact insolvent, including a federal state in search of new resources.

If one therefore considers the three key factors of the dislocation phase, we can see:

- That the EU is much less dependent on the "Dollar/Debt" base than the United States for example. Only some member states like the United Kingdom in particular (the Netherlands are also affected) are, but the heart of the Eurozone is only slightly affected.

- That the EU, and especially the Eurozone, is indeed very responsive to the factor of the great diversity of its constituent parts. If European States were so lacking in independence as American States it would be the guarantee of a widespread explosion of the EU.

But, and this is a key point, the functioning of the EU is very polycentric, not centralized. States have tremendous leeway. The ECB provides a consistent monetary framework. European Structural Funds provide long-term cohesion. And this polycentric system knows, as it has shown for over 50 years, how to be imaginative when the situation requires. Particularly since it knows it is fragile and the outcome of a pure and simple creation of the will of its people and leaders. And as regards the heavyweight of the Eurozone and the EU, Germany, at a time when its global markets are collapsing or risk closing, no price is too high to ensure that the Union European and the Eurozone remain privileged openings for German industry.

The problems of the EU and the Eurozone, that the crisis is going to reveal in broad daylight in the 2010-2020 decade, are in fact political. A Europe on autopilot, under the control of bureaucrats and lobbyists, is missing citizens and political leaders. It was widely noticed in 2009, with the absence or ineffectiveness of the EU on global issues: ridiculous posturing about bonuses and tax havens in the G20 without daring to put the Dollar issue on the table while the Eurozone suffers directly from its weakness, complete failure in Copenhagen where Europe, nevertheless a world leader in environmental matters, was not even been able to lead the discussions.

The previous generations of Europeans in fact contrived to build an outstanding ship, now welcoming five hundred million passengers on board, but so far they

option politically impossible to discuss in theory, but quite feasible in an emergency. This is one of the many paradoxes of the way the EU works. Source: Times, 15/02/2009

have failed to find a crew the size of this mega-liner. It continues to be steered by pilots of little boats or small cargo men who claim to be able to handle a huge boat, whilst they know nothing of the phenomena of inertia and the particular demands of advanced maneuvers that characterize the command of such a giant of the seas.

However, if there is a political entity today whose complexity and size are a remarkable scale model of global governance issues, it is the EU. And if there is really a region in the world that has more than ideas, but real practical experience, in terms of a new international currency, it is indeed the Eurozone. In short, only the Europeans have the real experience to reply to the two key questions of the coming decade, that is how to hand on global governance from a unipolar to a multipolar world and its monetary corollary, how to transform an international monetary system based on the currency of one country (the Dollar) into a system based on a currency made up of a basket of currencies.

That does not make the EU a better or superior player to the others. Nevertheless, that makes it a player which still has a completely legitimate claim to prepare and organize the global discussions on this subject. But obviously for that to happen, again the EU leaders would have to have the measure of the problem. It is hardly likely that they would have before the middle of the decade. France has no presidential elections before 2012 and Germany no parliamentary elections before 2013. In European affairs the United Kingdom will no longer count in the coming decade. First, because it is entangled in a historic economic crisis linked to the collapse of its principal backer since 1945 (the United States) and the shattering of Anglo-Saxon model that allowed London to have a disproportionate influence inside Europe as well as outside and, secondly, because it is the Eurozone, to which England will not belong until, at least, right at the end of the decade, which is now the engine and the architect of developments in major EU policies.

Really then it's the Eurozone leaders and their fellow citizens, who will or will not make the difference in the 2010-2020 decade. If, at the end of the first half of the decade, they are able to clearly state that Europe now intends to take on its global responsibilities by itself to try to find the paths that lead to the world after the crisis, and that, therefore, they are taking a new look at all the assumptions that have characterized recent decades (preferential transatlantic link, submission to the United States, etc.), then they are in a position to help the world (and their 500 million fellow citizens) reach a new stable world order between now and 2020.

Provided, of course, that they do not continue to think about the future as an extension of the past, that they do not continue to believe that one runs a continent in the middle of an historic crisis as one manages a region or a business[69] and that

---

[69] To compare the management of a political entity to that of a business is the very symbol of the reduction of political thought to a non-thought. It is the great victory of those who have led the world in the current crisis (financiers, bankers, oligarchs of all kinds) to have accomplished this sad feat. It's one of the pieces of good news brought by the global crisis that clearly shows that there is a need for political governance to guarantee the complex social balances in difficult times and to mediate on the long, medium and short term collective

they continue to recognize that with the EU we now have, we Europeans, the tools to forge our own destiny[70]. So it is with the arrival of the first generation born after the Treaty of Rome (1957) and the Erasmus generation (1987) that everything will be to play for in mid-decade.

Either the EU equips itself, naturally, with a new elite feeling completely at home in the European environment, thus also naturally developing the European position in the global game and, at the same time, bringing forth a trans-European civil society and political parties to run the politics of the continent. Or the EU will "give" itself a dangerous mix of bureaucrats and xenophobic parties, which will push our continent in the direction of a national Europeanist bloc that will perfectly fit the scenario of the tragic end of the "world before" and conflicts between regional blocs.

In this regard, we must be aware that the xenophobic and ultra-nationalist movements in various European countries have more in common than their apparent national rhetoric might suggest. Indeed, the discussion on "France for the French", "Italy for the Italians", "Holland for the Dutch", etc. is easily summed up with a generic slogan "Europe for Europeans". And one doesn't need to be a genius to see that for at least a decade, this trend is asserting itself in Europe. These movements are in regular contact with each other. Proponents of the "West" fighting against barbarism[71] (usually equated with everybody who doesn't agree with them) are among the forces that discreetly encourage these developments by their direct actions (enlistment for conflicts like Iraq, Afghanistan, etc.) or their arguments on immigration, religion or foreigners.

Behind the current European leaders a European generation is rising up which has its political roots in post-war Europe, in the "Western" vision of the Europe of Mussolini, Hitler, Petain or Franco, to which those nostalgic of Stalinism attach themselves without difficulty as well. These "grandsons" of the European dictators of the 1930s have only two major differences with their ancestors, first they are dressed in suits and ties and no longer in military uniforms (the "net book" in the hand serves their purposes for a highly controlled society much better than the pistol stuck in the belt), second, they are not anti-Semitic, on the contrary, they have even become pro-Zionist. It is not so much their interest for the future of the Israeli people or the reality of their feelings about someone who is not one of them

---

choices. Not only is business management unable to take the long term into account because it's not profitable but, in addition, it is overwhelmingly incapable of taking into account that which is not immediately quantifiable and which, in the history of people, is often the crux of the matter.

[70] We will not forge it alone, of course, but with others. However, today's Europe, for the little it dares to say out loud what it thinks itself, is able to be a player of global influence, independent and an engine, which has not happened for seventy years, since 1940.

[71] In power today in Washington, London, Paris, Rome, The Hague, Copenhagen, Berlin

(white, European Christians for the most part[72]). It's just that they have realized that with this type of declaration of faith, they have shaken off one of the main signs of right-wing extremism in Europe, and at the same time they have gained easy access to the major pro-Israel media especially the U.S. media which "makes up" much of the European press (for a decade the latter satisfies itself with copying or translating U.S. articles[73]).

For those with few scruples, believing that the end always justifies the means, it is a very good political performance indeed. Racism with complete impunity and media access guaranteed for the price of a single mass (so to speak). From Gianfranco Fini, to Eric Besson via Brice Hortefeux, Geerd Wilders, de Wever and others, the national-Europeanists are a rising force in European politics in the 2010-2020 decade[74].

And numerous bureaucrats who are at the heart of the current system of European Union governance (Brussels officials and officials from the major national ministries) have basically no problem with the vision of a European nationalism which would ensure the continuation of the process of European integration while avoiding the questioning of their powers and privileges. The leaders of these populist and xenophobic movements have, when the day arrives, no problem in refraining from any action against the EU bureaucracy even if they cram their speeches with attacks against the "Europe of Brussels".

After 2014, which will see the first European election with real trans-European divisions, particularly including the assertion of a national-Europeanist vision, the leaders of these parties will make do really well with the system in place if it allows them to initiate their ideas of a closed Europe and controlled populations. Moreover, with their political ascendancy, they could not care less for democracy. Breeding shows!

What are will we be facing? A multitude of small national parties (because a national party is still small on the scale of 500 million EU citizens), continuing to

---

[72] Just like the U.S. evangelists (who in general greatly appreciate them) who have only made a common cause with Zionist groups in the United States because of a common opposition to Islam and the Arab world. In fact the latter wish for the creation of the Greater Israel since its advent signifies the imminence of Armageddon, and thus the destruction of Israel. With friends like these, the people of Israel no longer needs enemies.

[73] The French version of Slate, created by former Le Monde staff is a leading example. And Le Monde itself now fills many of its pages with translated U.S. articles. Paris has really become a provincial town where even opinions are imported from the U.S. metropolis.

[74] Since 1998 I have tried to draw attention to this political risk by writing a forecast called "EU 2009: when the grandsons of Hitler, Pétain, Franco, Mussolini and Stalin take control of the EU". This work only had some impact after Le Pen's success in the second round of the 2002 French presidential elections. The current crisis only reinforces the trend identified from the end of the 1990s because it weakens the social fabric, faith in democracy and trust in the political, economic and intellectual elite.

claim that there are no European issues, and that, consequently, the European elections are essentially national ballots. Small national parties served by the media who will continue to claim that European issues do not interest people[75]. All this for one essential reason: the political leaders of our countries have no tangible political experience of the Europeans (and therefore voters in a European election[76]); for them Europe is limited to summits and ceremonies.

Basically, as far as our leaders are concerned, a citizen of another EU country is a "foreigner just like another", no more significant than an American, a Russian or Chinese. And for good reason, he has no electoral impact on them, even if by his vote he clearly has a political impact, directly influencing the composition of the European Parliament or the European Council. But to care about a political impact it must be a man or a woman in politics bearing a project, a political vision and not simply a candidate for election duties.

What is certain in any case is that it is not the multitude of uncoordinated national parties that will be able to effectively oppose the rise of the national-Europeanist movement. They are generally unable to prevent the rise of extremism in their own national environment and are directly responsible for increasing voter apathy. Moreover, they appear as accomplices of the financial interests that generated the current crisis. Not only cannot the national parties oppose the rise of antidemocratic forces, but one can even say that they are responsible for their emergence. Without a trans-European political force promoting the democratization of the EU and its role as a constructive force of influence at global level, particularly to get through the current crisis, Europe will directly contribute to the implementation of the tragic scenario and direct conflict between competing blocs.

The arrival of these new generations born in Europe will certainly lead to the formation of a trans-European movement promoting the democratization of the EU and an active global role for Europe being a kind of European democratic front. I myself am working to that end. But for now, this trend is far less powerful than the other.

Serving no particular interest, it has all the legitimacy and the weakness of collective causes that everyone finds so obvious and that few people get involved in until the day when everyone realizes that it may be already too late. As Europeans, it would be presumptuous to think that a crisis of the magnitude we are experiencing doesn't reserve some very unpleasant surprises in terms of democracy

---

75 While referenda on the constitution in France and the Netherlands have provided ample evidence to the contrary.

76 A voter is not the same, it depends on the election in which he participates. His subjects of interest vary. In a municipal election he will focus on topics unrelated to those which decide their vote in a national election. It's exactly the same scenario for the European elections except that no political leader starts to talk about the issues that would motivate him as a European voter.

and peace. Oscar Wilde pointed to experience as the name that men give to the sum of their errors. If we Europeans can share our experience with the world, it is primarily because we have made many mistakes. This decade will be a test on the matter. Have we learned from our mistakes and, therefore, can we use our experience to benefit everyone? Or really have we learned nothing from our mistakes and are preparing ourselves to make the same mistakes as in the past with simply more modern clothes?

To conclude this analysis of the EU in the coming decade, I would remind the reader, especially Europea, of a fact that we tend to forget, trapped between our current national leaders' narrow chauvinism and U.S. media propaganda. The only continent that has exported, retail as well as wholesale, political models for over two thousand years (the time of ancient Greece), is Europe. Democracy, nation-state, communism, totalitarianism, etc. the best and worst regimes of these last centuries have all come from a European intellectual and conceptual strain. The United States is a plain descendant of our ideas as was the USSR too, or the Chinese Communist Party. It is not a matter of making an unseemly display, but it is a case of not forgetting who we are[77] in order to be what we hope for.

Russia is better prepared than the others for this historic transition

With a second decade of power for Vladimir Putin (whether as Prime Minister or President), Russia is, a priori, guaranteed a sustained period of central government stability. Gas and oil revenues (which will not experience a significant lasting downturn again compared to 2009 average prices) enable it to plan its strategic development internally and externally. The opening of the first Russian high-speed train between Moscow and St. Petersburg at the end of December 2009 has opened what will be a decade of strong transport infrastructure modernization, including oil and gas pipelines.

Competing projects, designed to "bypass" Russia, like Nabucco, are fizzling out because without active U.S. political and financial support they drift slowly but surely towards the simple economic logic that leads to reintegrate Russia to them. The 2010 opening of the first Russian oil terminal on the Pacific coast (only two terminals, on the Baltic and Black Sea, existed until now) will allow the country to fully involve itself in Asian growth for years to come. This is also the great challenge of this transitional decade for the Kremlin. To be able to benefit from the dynamism of Asia without being jostled by the Asians, and especially the Chinese,

---

[77] And this comment is, of course, equally valid for the most obscure aspects of our European identity.

increasingly present in Siberia, and ensure a strong strategic relationship with the EU all whilst keeping European claims on Russia's future at arm's length[78]

France has a key role to play in EU-Russia relations for the years between 2010 and 2020. The directional movement of the Russian elite to Paris and the Cote d'Azur isn't only a small detail in the matter. It reflects an historical reality for both countries, each located at an extremity of the European continent: all European balance is impossible without them... and without, of course, the third scoundrel, Germany, at the center of this same continent. French and Germans together occupy the greater part of Russian imagination when it comes to the "West" and they have a force of attraction and unique partnership from Moscow's perspective. But that is only true on the express condition that this European interest is indeed the EU's and not a puppet from Washington or elsewhere.

The memorable refusal of France, Germany and Russia[79] to be drawn into the war and the historical lie of the invasion of Iraq in 2002/2003 is a good example of the type of global level structured partnerships that Europeans and Russians can orchestrate if they find common goals. There is one that Russia has put on the table of potential negotiations since the G20 London Summit, replacing the Dollar as the international benchmark currency. It is in Euroland's clear interest to undertake such a step in order to bring a halt to the current world monetary chaos.

If France actually had leaders with a real strategic vision and a sense of history, like De Gaulle and Mitterrand had, there is no doubt that the French government would have already prompted the EU to take this opportunity to discuss it with Moscow, and the EU would be the special guest at the next BRIC Summit. We will have to wait until after 2012 to see if such an opportunity will be taken. Failing which, Europeans will be responsible for the continuing downward spiral into hell of the global monetary system in the second half of the decade, paving the way for a Russian repositioning in Asian thinking.

Remember that Moscow has twice successfully prevented imperial domination of Europe by contributing decisively to the defeat of Napoleon and Hitler and that in the 1930s Stalin had tried unsuccessfully to convince France and the United Kingdom to form an alliance with the USSR against Nazi Germany. The fear of Communism prevented such an alliance which would nevertheless have spared Europe a suicidal war and several decades' division. The 2010s will enable the new European elite to be tested to see if they can overcome their fear of anti-

---

[78] A prominent member of the Russian Academy of Sciences admirably summarized the dilemma by saying: "In the twenty-first century, either we manage our relationship with Brussels effectively, or we will fall under Beijing's influence". Behind the sometimes very provocative Kremlin statements there is, in effect, a deep conviction that a strong partnership can be forged with the West. It is for Europeans and these two key partners, the French and Germans, to harness it properly.

[79] It is, moreover, a good example of what European participation in a BRIC summit could bring in a very constructive way.

Americanism to forecast a global monetary disaster and its attendant disastrous consequences.

One thing is certain, already in the 1930s, it was unwise to listen to advice from financial and banking circles if one was concerned about the common good in the medium and long term. The Russian elite are not very gifted at anticipating European emotional reactions to some of their statements or actions which are particularly forceful. Scaremongering does not lead very far when looking for reliable partners. In this regard, French, Germans and Europeans in general have an important educational role to play. In any case, Russia is a good candidate for a less volatile decade than the other major powers. The fact that it has already passed through its own chaotic transition period, the 1990s, contributes significantly. In effect, it has already been involved in the "world after" for over twenty years, since the fall of the Berlin Wall.

China, when the provincial cousin
becomes one of the big bosses

This title may seem disrespectful to China, yet I do not think it is in the sense that it accurately describes the developments taking place for Chinese power. Within a generation or less, Chinese leaders have actually gone from being provincial - to whom integration into the world order designed by Washington was proposed in exchange for beads (Treasury Bonds and U.S. Dollars) - to the status of a major economic and financial power on which the future developments in the world largely depend. This situation is often the theme of comic films, but in this case it will more likely take on a dramatic shape as and when the magnitude of "the scam" is unveiled (and that's the whole Sino-American drama of the first half of this decade).

Of course the big winner of the decade will be Beijing. Everybody knows now[80]. But as so often in history, the question is what will the price of this victory be? Indeed, there is no doubt about the general trend. The 2000s was marked by the irresistible rise of China first in the economic and commercial fields, then in the financial and monetary arena. The 2010 decade will be one of the first uses of these new powers by Beijing and coupled with it, the price to pay for their use.

To take a rather trivial example, ten years ago Beijing was a sort of "provincial cousin" which went to the city where the United States in particular had "unloaded" everything it could (Dollars, U.S. Treasury Bonds, agency securities such as Fannie Mae, Freddie Mac, etc.) in exchange for its good value products. In ten years China will be the first industrial, economic, commercial and financial

---

[80] Even if we distrust the evidence.

power in the world and the "country cousin" will become the "big boss". The nature of the process that will lead to this transformation will play out in the first half of this decade. We can even exactly forecast the area that will determine this outcome. It is that of Chinese financial reserves and thus the Dollar/Yuan exchange rate and U.S. Treasury Bonds[81]. Directly, the Europeans carry little weight, except to threaten the flow of Chinese exports to the EU. But it is a dangerous weapon to use, except to have a clear strategy as regards the Dollar and the future international monetary system, which the EU is really devoid of today. In effect, it is the United States who holds the key to this outcome.

Very simply, either they convince the Chinese by their actions that they haven't taken them for idiots in recent years and, therefore, that their Dollars and Treasury Bonds have a firm value for years to come, or they oblige Chinese leaders to lose face in front of their people because of the collapse in value of China's reserves due to the downfall of the Dollar and sharp drop in Treasury Bonds. In the first case, Beijing will be placed at the centre of a virtuous circle of effective power seeking to skillfully manage the transition of the world before the crisis to the world after. In the second case, China will have no other choice but to try to limit its losses by any means and severely punish the offense.

At the beginning of the decade, after the G20 failure in London to begin a discussion on the Dollar, and because of the Western refusal to discuss it in any forum whatsoever, the scales unfortunately are currently tilting towards the second scenario. Beijing's accelerated march towards Asian regional integration is a sure sign. The January 2010 opening of the free trade zone linking Beijing and the ASEAN is a crucial step, as is the strengthened partnership with Tokyo which, this decade, will work to create a kind of EU inspired Asian Union. Asia like Latin America for that matter, has a diversity compatible with European style regional integration, many states, core sharing of powerful common cultural factors (particularly the trio of China-Japan-Korea), economic complementarities (countries at different stages of economic development), similar geopolitical challenges[82].

But at the same time, Chinese leaders will also have to face the challenge of their own ambitions and the other big Chinese issue of the 2010 decade: is Chinese growth compatible with the rest of the world? The answer to this question will

---

[81] With more than 2 Trillion Dollars of reserves, nearly two-thirds in U.S. Treasury Bonds and Dollars, China has accumulated a "prosperity" that closely depends on the value of the U.S. currency and the health of the United States economy. These are two illusions that the crisis is making vanish before the eyes of leaders in Beijing. This explains why, first in 2009, they began to stop buying new U.S. debt and, secondly, in 2010, to sell their holdings of United States Treasury Bonds to diversify their reserves into the Euro, gold, oil, commodities and businesses, especially European and American

[82] This raises the great dilemma of India, on the edge of this Asian group, and a link with other areas including the Islamic world and the Middle East. India, like Turkey or Iran, are countries which, to be themselves, must probably build themselves as links between other large areas and must refuse to be absorbed by one or the other, with all the potential for conflict that this entails in the 2010-2020 decade.

unfold in two stages. First of all, will Chinese growth of between 8% and 10% that claims to have succeeded in keeping Beijing's leaders in power despite the crisis thanks to a huge plan to support the economy survive the test of reality?

Because, for the moment, it is only a matter of official statistics, largely unreliable as all official statistics in a time of crisis (think of wartime military press releases, there are only victories or at worst organized retreats to prepared positions, never defeats, routs and disarray so common as conflicts unfold). It is certain that current growth is more than 70% due to public spending. It is unlikely that the rest of the world (certainly not the United States, in any event, where the consumer will remain insolvent for the whole decade) would be able to take on a major share of this growth in the future because now everyone wants to export and everyone has his finger on the protectionist trigger.

Only the Chinese and Asian consumer is then left to enable the leaders in Beijing keep the head of their economy above water. In the best case scenario, that will prove to be very difficult in the first half of this decade, leading to high social and regional tensions. Beijing will, therefore, have to be even heavier handed than in the past to control public opinion. The Chinese government will struggle to resist Chinese and/or Asian nationalism to do so[83].

Any sign from the United States indicating that the value of China's reserves is threatened by a falling dollar and U.S. Treasury Bonds will act as a detonator. The absolute requirement of 2010/2011 is therefore, to actually show that Beijing is finding a place that suits it in international organizations. And on this subject, France and the EU can weigh in decisively to free up the place by themselves (number of votes) to compel the United States and Japan to do likewise. Otherwise Beijing, with the other BRICs and the rest of Asia, will be driven to build its "alternative world order" creating the ideal conditions for a major economic, commercial and military global confrontation.

Still, if one considers, on the one hand, the huge uncertainties weighing on the reality and/or the sustainability of Chinese growth generated in 2009 by the government's recovery plan and, on the other, the inevitability of the Dollar's fall against the Yuan and the loss in value of U.S. Treasury Bonds, it becomes quite clear that Chinese leaders will face a decade far more difficult than we imagine in general and even than what the majority of the Chinese leaders imagine.

The compatibility of China's growth with the rest of the world is, therefore, really the heart of the dilemma:

---

[83] At present Beijing has already given instructions to its industry to systematically favour Asian suppliers rather than their American or European counterparts when possible (and that is increasingly often), another development that illustrates how much Europeans and Americans are deluding themselves if they think that Chinese growth (if maintained) will save their economies.

- If this growth exists and causes the rise in power of an Asian bloc centered on Beijing, it will significantly increase all the falling trends in each of the major regions of the world[84] and thus eventually a mentality of confrontation between economic and political blocs. It is Europe in 1913 at world level. Sadly, we can guess the sequel.

- If this growth does not exist, and in fact from 2010/2011, China is unable to quickly substitute its domestic demand for lost exports, the United States will face a sudden collapse of its currency and an unprecedented budget crisis because Beijing can no longer (and will no longer) absorb U.S. Dollars and Treasury Bonds. The world monetary system "will go over the edge" at the same time, leading to complete monetary, financial, economic and social chaos, causing an even sharper rise in regional blocs' power than in the previous case and furthermore an acceleration of belligerent forces' coming to power.

Therefore, there only remains the option of growth that would be real and used by China to stimulate the global economy, particularly those of Europe and the United States. So, we go back to square one on the basic responsibility of the Sino-American pair in the first half of the 2010-2010 decade. In view of the United States' progress, reasons for optimism are quite low.

The only hope would be that the Europeans, basically the Germans, Spaniards, Italians, Poles, Dutch and British (not the French because the current French president is not seen as credible either in Washington or Beijing) put pressure on Washington to prevent the United States continuing to play the political weakening of the dollar to dump their debt for next to nothing. An era is over for the United States and only the Europeans can get that message over to Washington (if that's possible[85]).

But Chinese Communist Party leaders are certainly under no illusion. They know that if they turn in the direction of the tragic path to the future, they will be subjected to the double ordeal of external confrontations with other regional blocs, as well as the domestic risk of social chaos and regional outburst. Europeans, unlike Americans with whom Beijing is engaged in a zero sum game, can help Chinese leaders to take a buoyant future path, that of a reconstruction of global governance. Provided, of course, that the Europeans agree to act completely independently.

---

[84] And, bad news for the environment, in this context one can forget any attempt to control the spread of pollution worldwide.

[85] And I saw that myself at a high-level seminar held in Washington in 2005 where as Europeans, we were able to pass a sharp message on the growing disconnect between U.S. policies of the time and international realities. Not only is it time for Europe to speak to the United States with a single voice, but it is urgent that this be done harshly so that the U.S. elite can see that even we (!) have realized that the little world built by the West is falling apart.

Japan and Taiwan, two examples of the emergence of an Asian bloc around Beijing between now and 2015

If summer 2009 doesn't seem to have experienced major geopolitical crises such as the Russian-Georgian conflict in summer 2008 or the one between Israel and Hezbollah in summer 2006, it would nevertheless be wrong to infer that nothing of strategic importance happened this summer. Quite the contrary, two pivotal events took place in Asia between June and September 2009. They will have a medium and long term influence on the world's advance and, from 2010 affect the current global imbalances, military as well as financial and economic. In any event, they constitute the premise of global geopolitical dislocation.

The world of the systemic crisis is in fact a world of imbalances and of chaotic redistribution. Thus, these events in summer 2009 illustrate Asia's rapid shift outside the geopolitical order inherited from the Second World War, that is to say:

- Japan's "true orange revolution"

- China's "tranquil satellization" of Taiwan

Japan's "true orange revolution"

The 2000s were marked by a series of revolutions called "orange" modeled on the Ukraine's confrontation between pro-Russian power and pro-Western opponents in 2004. These events subsequently inspired similarly labeled efforts in Belarus and Georgia. Japan, without confrontation and without claiming such a label has, however, fulfilled a similar process, ending 60 years of domination by the same political party. The fact that this party was pro-Western and a faithful Washington intermediary since the Second World War doesn't change the fact that without rotation of power a democracy is only a political fiction and that the Japanese have just pulled down this fiction as in any good revolution.

If Japan were not one of the world's major economic powers, the second largest holder of Dollar reserves and U.S. Treasury Bonds on the planet and, in general, one of the "USA trimaran's" two floats (the other being the United Kingdom), this "orange revolution" could be considered purely a Japanese domestic political issue. But, of course, this is not the case. It is, on the contrary, a major geopolitical event that marks a historic turning point as much for Japan's overall strategic direction as for U.S. influence in Asia but also, a crucial aspect at this time of world economic and financial crisis, of the United States' ability to finance their growing deficits and avoid a Dollar collapse.

Because the DPJ (Democratic Party of Japan), which now completely dominates both houses and the country's executive, has posted three clear objectives which mark a break with the past six decades of the country's strategic positioning[86]:

- Reconciliation with China and the rest of Asia.
- End of the weak Yen policy
- End of the automatic purchase of U.S. Treasury Bonds

Far from being ideological goals, these objectives are the result of internal requirements, which are at the heart of this party's electoral victory. The Japanese have had enough of a power which favored the interests of the country's large exporting firms and those of the U.S. major strategic partner to the detriment of their own. Or, to put it differently and perhaps in a more revealing fashion on the strategic impact of the current crisis, the socio-economic consequences of this present crisis has made a large majority of Japanese aware that the interests of their major exporters and those (converging) of the « American big brother » were no longer the same as theirs.

The DPJ's landslide victory is, therefore, a requirement for any radical change in the foundations of Japanese politics in recent decades. The Japanese want their money and efforts to benefit themselves and their children rather than shareholders in Sony, Toyota or Toshiba and the United States government and consumers. They understood that China is their preferred economic partner of the future (about to become the country's principal trading partner ahead of the United States this year) and that their relationships with their region, Asia, are now a priority.

The new Japanese government is therefore compelled, whatever Washington thinks, to implement the triple severance mentioned above. It will try to do it diplomatically, but there really is no other choice except to suffer a devastating electoral backlash. And, due to the crisis, it really doesn't have much time in front of it. Yukio Hatoyama, the new Prime Minister, knows very well that he must show results to the Japanese public from 2010. That's to say letting the yen rise and stop buying excess U.S. Treasury Bonds.

For some years the United States has only had two faithful allies in monetary and financial affairs, the United Kingdom and Japan[87]. Without brutal reconsideration (which is not the way the Japanese do things), summer 2009 would have, however, marked the demise of one of two faithful allies. And considering that the United States' last "float" is the United Kingdom (the "sick man of Europe"), one can gauge how inevitable and close the U.S. wreck has become.

---

[86] We will not dwell here on the direct military implications of the change in power such as the decision to halt Japanese aid to provision the U.S. army in the ambit of its commitments in Iraq and Afghanistan.

[87] For example, last July (latest figures available), only these two countries had increased their holdings of U.S. debt, while the other large holders (Russia, China, oil producing States) were sellers.

China's "tranquil satellization" of Taiwan

One price that the United States will have to pay to avoid China causing a sudden collapse of the Dollar is the (re) integration of Taiwan with the "mother-land". The summer of 2009 marked a visible acceleration of such a process that can be called the "tranquil satellization" of Taiwan, like the so-called communist "satellite states" outside the USSR. No conflict here either. Would East Asia become the follower of quiet revolutions? Or, has the Middle Kingdom's power of attraction already become irresistible on the basis of U.S. economic collapse?

The fact is that Beijing has in recent months become the country's primary partner in terms of investment and foreign trade, while the People's Republic has embarked on a massive charm offensive in terms of humanitarian aid. Chinese leaders have even explicitly announced that they would willingly support Taiwanese industry to prevent it from collapsing under the impact of its falling exports. Thus they asked many mainland Chinese companies to replace their foreign suppliers with Taiwanese companies for a sum in excess of 10 billion Euros while offering bank loans to businesses on the island.

Against the background of a political power now more conciliatory towards Beijing[88], progress is rapid and impressive. Taiwanese leaders have boldly stated that these changes do not alter their refusal to (re) integrate with China. Actually, the reality is that now their economy is heavily dependent on mainland China, the first destination for their exports, the largest source of trade surpluses, and now investors increasingly "authorized" on the island.

An informal handover of Taiwan by the United States to China seems to be well underway. At the speed U.S. weakening is taking place, set against a backdrop of growing Chinese power, between now and the end of the decade Taiwan will have found a status as special province like Hong Kong or its equivalent. And all this without war or U.S. military intervention.

The creation in 2010 of the free trade agreement between China and ASEAN countries is a further illustration of the speedy establishment of an "Asian bloc" around China. And so, even Taiwan's trade relations with its ASEAN neighbors (formerly the preserve of Washington) now take place thanks to Beijing's goodwill.

---

[88] There is no question of a referendum on the island's independence.

Latin America, so close to becoming an innovative international player, but so close to the U.S

The 2000s saw Latin America achieve one of the most remarkable transformations in its history. In a way it could be compared to the period which, exactly two hundred years ago, saw the subcontinent liberate itself from Spanish colonial rule in the 1810-1820 decade. This time it would be a matter of freeing itself from the overwhelming influence of the United States. That's what the 2000-2010 decade has brought, except in Colombia where, on the contrary, the influence of the United States has increased. Two contrary major geopolitical trends will mark the next decade in Latin America.

The regional integration process towards a Latin American Union having economic, customs, monetary and political size will continue and probably accelerate. Brazil and Argentina are the engines as well as Venezuela and Cuba. The influence of one or the other will decide it as more or less opposed to the United States. But it is the United States itself which will be the key factor in the global positioning of the sub-continent, partner or adversary of the United States. "Poor Latin America, so far from God and so close to the United States" one could say parodying Porfirio Dias, the early twentieth century dictator of Mexico when speaking of his country.

Indeed, in the context of international withdrawal of U.S. power, Latin America belongs to Washington's "back yard history". From the Monroe Doctrine of the nineteenth century to the "Big Stick" of the twentieth century, the United States' first steps as an imperial power were taken on Latin America territory. Rich in raw materials, the sub-continent is a vast growth market that Washington doesn't want to see slip out of its orbit permanently, even more than the Middle East oil producing states. The recent reactivation of the U.S. military command for Latin America (abolished in 1950) such as the installation of new military bases in Colombia are clear signs that Washington intends to make a powerful comeback to the game in Latin America[89].

The next presidential elections in Brazil (end 2010) and Argentina (2011) will serve as benchmarks because rumors are increasing of the risks of electoral connivance to allow a return to power of Washington's allies. Given the painful history of Latin American countries regarding dictatorships supported by its big Northern neighbour, it would be naive to sweep these possibilities under the carpet as common conspiracy theories.

---

[89] The overthrow of Honduras President, who signed the ALBA (Bolivarian Alliance for the Americas created by Venezuela, Cuba and Bolivia), by a military junta without serious condemnation of the event by Washington has been perceived as a thunderbolt throughout the region, marking the return of the "Big Stick".

Now, everyone knows that in the second half of the twentieth century Latin America has been a theater of deadly plots woven in Washington. The real question is not whether Washington will try to regain some control of affairs in Latin America over the next decade, but to what extent the United States still has the means to do so. The process of the subcontinent's regional integration probably offers the best protection and the best barometer of such outside intervention. Indeed, it is under the impetus of leaders rather opposed or at least having little enthusiasm for the U.S. model that integration has progressed strongly in the past decade. UNASUR, the Union of South American Nations, has been, since 2008, the most "all-encompassing" format because all of Latin America meets there.

Mercosur continues to be the most economically integrated process and the most powerful regional engine because the two regional economic powers, Brazil and Argentina, meet there. The abandonment of the Americas free trade zone project, dear to Washington's heart (to create a partnership between NAFTA and UNASUR), with the United States focusing on the marginalization of Venezuela, Bolivia and Cuba at the centre of the UNASUR process, corresponds to a realistic and probably effective development of U.S. policy in the region. On the other hand, the attempt to influence the subcontinent's electoral process (which, if confirmed, will be visible from 2010-2011), will lead to a radicalization of both sides and to economic and military confrontations. Venezuela's Chavez is not Castro's Cuba: with oil it has advantages on a completely different scale and the world of 2010-2020 is nothing like that, under control, of the Cold War.

Finally, for Latin America, the other major feature of the next decade will be the growing assertion of the power of the indigenous population. If that will also operate against U.S. influence, no doubt it will severely restrict European influence and instead push the subcontinent towards Asia in particular, which is still virgin territory for modern common history.

Africa, more suitors and little hope

The 2010-2020 decade will again put Africa at the centre of global conflicts of interest. The race for raw materials, minerals, energy and agriculture will increase and thus make Africa a major issue for Europeans, North Americans, Asians and Latin Americans. Frankly it seems unlikely that Africans can play against this fierce competition in their collective interest. In effect, the 2000-2010 decade will not allow a significant number of new African leaders to emerge, dedicated to their people rather than their bank accounts, while the continent's potential elite continue to migrate to Europe, America or Asia.

Caught in a pincer-like grip between heightened religious conflicts (particularly the growing competition between Islam and Christianity) and the world powers' battles for influence, the possibility of sustaining a continental African identity through the African Union, or even only regional based just around South Africa, will really remain difficult throughout the next ten years. The economic crisis will help to divert the interest of nations giving aid to Africa towards the concerns of domestic poverty.

Ethnic conflicts can't be stopped whilst the international community, particularly France and the United Kingdom, has not agreed to launch, with the Africans[90] of course, an extensive process of reorganizing national borders in Africa. These legacies of the colonial era are at the heart of all conflicts devastating the continent for decades. The further away from the colonial period, the further these boundaries are bizarre and disconnected from the reality of the people they are supposed to embody as boundary stones of nation-states. Public or private aid to Africa will continue to be of no earthly sse whilst the main problem is not addressed.

Yet neither in Africa, France nor the United Kingdom can one perceive the slightest political trend today which would allow one to hope for such a political (r)evolution coming to serve Africans. The only certainty is that, in the case of increased conflicts between large regional blocs, Africa will become the front line for direct confrontations even more deadly than in a scenario of the emergence of a sustainable new world order. In addition, a question remains open, will China limit itself to an ultra active economic and commercial presence, or will it surrender, like other powers before it, to the idea of direct colonization?

Middle East and the Muslim world
The more things happen, the less it changes

The "enfant terrible" of the 2000s will remain, with Africa, the other player missing from the 2010-2020 decade. Or more accurately, it will once again be forced to exist only by reacting. Taken apart by U.S. invasions ("out and out" invasions in Iraq and Afghanistan, "velvet" invasions in Saudi Arabia, the Gulf countries, Egypt, Morocco, etc.), torn by internal and inter-ethnic conflicts between Muslims (Shiite/Sunni), corrupted by oil money, paralyzed by the Israeli-Palestinian conflict, the Middle East will continue to be the front line of direct confrontation between the major powers. The downfall of U.S. power, protective of many regimes in the region, will cause further instability throughout the decade.

---

[90] But in this case it is people, not leaders - most of whom remain as a result of rigged elections, or a key country like South Africa, which has the democratic legitimacy and necessary influence to stimulate such a geopolitical transformation of Africa.

The real risk of nuclear strikes related to a direct conflict with Israel (especially if Israel feels in a position to lose by conventional means), the risk of regional conflict in case of pre-emptive strike on Iranian facilities, through the Saudi Arabia and Egypt whose governments are sitting on powerful social and therefore fundamentalist[91] time- bombs, the region will continue its chaotic journey through the early twenty-first century. As for Africa, if the world turns to the tragic scenario of conflict between large blocs, the Middle East and its energy wealth will be one of the direct and significant issues of international confrontations.

Dubai, a kind of regional emblem, going from best to worst in 2008-2009, will become a destination for adventure tourism, to visit the first city in history which consists of ghost skyscrapers. But the Middle East also has three key countries which are not Arab: Israel, Turkey and Iran. Their development will play a significant role in the future of the region, but also for the world in the decade we are just starting. Iran's case will be more specifically addressed in another chapter of this book devoted to the issue of nuclear proliferation.

Israel 2020, two scenarios
Towards the end of the state of Israel, or towards a lasting Israeli state

I have chosen to write about Israel's future by adapting the two 2020 scenarios on this subject, which I developed with LEAP from 2006 onwards. In addition they are, in my opinion, very practical and well documented and these last four years have confirmed their logic, they offer the opportunity to "polish" the anticipation process at the heart of this book.

Thus, the 2010-2020 decade is probably the most important in the still short history of the state of Israel. It involves, in fact, Israel urgently redefining a new strategy because in these last decades Jewish state's tactics has been mainly to rely on the unconditional support of U.S. omnipotence. Yet, the 2010-2020 years will see this non-conditionality as well as this omnipotence fade away. Attempts to replace the U.S. option by a "Western" option involving the Europeans more closely[92], making Israel the forward outpost of a West in conflict with the Arab-Muslim world, will suffer the same fate, even if they can give the illusion of it working until the middle of this decade.

---

[91]The fundamentalists' success in the region, as elsewhere, is essentially due to the huge social inequalities in these countries and the endemic poverty of a majority of the population. The United States and Europe will be able to see it directly in the 2010-2020 decade with the emergence of major domestic terrorism fed by these same causes, poverty and inequality.

[92] But still under U.S. supervision.

It is certainly the Lebanese-Israeli crisis of summer 2006 that helped pinpoint the parameters that will now define the Middle East regional rules. The development of the two scenarios thus includes the often radical transformation of seven strategic parameters since the conflict of the summer of 2006 (and the bombing of Gaza in autumn 2008 has only legitimized the parameters used). Either scenario then results on the nature of the responses of key players to the changes in their strategic environment. The first sets out the consequences, in the radically new environment that emerged from the crisis of summer 2006, continuing the policy adopted by Israel since the mid 90s for another decade and a half.

The second explores the potential of a radical break in Israeli policy with that followed in recent years, to adapt to the new constraints weighing on the Middle East.
Seven strategic parameters have therefore been retained to provide the setting for these two scenarios:

- **Founding forces are now exhausted**
  The creation of the State of Israel is the result of two major trends characteristic of the period immediately after the Second World War, now in the course of extinction or completely snuffed out, that's to say, first, the general feeling of the West's guilt over the genocide of the Jewish people perpetrated by the Nazis and, secondly, the colonial model. The first trend, which is weakening rapidly with the increasing historical distance from its originating event, is a key factor in the creation of the state of Israel which was in fact considered by the West as an attempt to compensate for the atrocities committed against the Jewish people in Europe[93] between 1930 and 1945. The second trend, which virtually disappeared after decolonization, fundamentally influenced the choice of the place to establish the state of Israel in that it allowed "a piece of land to be carved out" on lands administered by the Europeans in colonial style.

- **The end of the period of a "dominant" military**
  The historical period of Israeli "dominance" in relation to its immediate Middle Eastern environment ended with the Israeli-Lebanese crisis of summer 2006. This period opened with the Israeli victory in the Six Day War of 1967 and was based in particular on two hypotheses now obsolete, the invincibility of the Israeli army and the omnipotence of the U.S. ally. The inability of the Israeli army to achieve the objectives that it had set itself at the start of the conflict in summer 2006 as well as Hezbollah's ability to effectively oppose the Israeli army has pushed back Israeli power to a degree of regional normalcy[94]. The

---

[93] The recent proliferation of ceremonies, films and other books on this theme, produced mainly by Jewish communities in Europe and the United States, is thus an attempt to halt the inexorable phenomenon of increasing historical distance.

[94] Even if there is no doubt that the Israeli army remains the most powerful army in the region.

inability of the U.S. ally to intervene militarily in the conflict, such as blocking UN resolutions calling for the early termination of the Israeli offensive, have confirmed the United States' significant weakening in the region. This situation helps to even more strongly weaken the concept of Israeli "dominance" because it was very closely linked to the feeling of total support by a U.S. power, itself overpowering. The United Nations' questioning of the Israeli army's actions vis-à-vis Palestinian civilians in Gaza, following the attack in 2008, is another example of the changing times.

- **The end of the unilateral option**
The strategic choices made by Israeli leaders since the assassination of Yitzhak Rabin, especially by the Prime Ministers Netanyahu, Sharon, Olmert and Netanyahu again, of using this "dominance" to try to impose unilateral solutions on regional problems, led to hasten the end of this period of "dominance". It is probable that, like many leaders in history, the latter have themselves fallen into the trap of "believing their own press releases" and overestimated the capabilities of their own forces. It is always the case that the systematic use of the military to establish and implement their policies, instead of dialogue and negotiation, has created a situation that has helped weaken that same military and strengthen their opponents' desire to be able to oppose it[95].

- **Strengthening opponents' military strategic capacity**
The Arab-Muslim world as a whole has constantly improved its ability to fight against U.S. military strategies and tactics, or be directly inspired by them (as in the case of the Israeli offensive in summer 2006). In fact for several years now, the conflicts in Afghanistan and Iraq provide daily lessons on the subject which are analyzed and disseminated throughout the Arab- Muslim world. The Israeli army's strategic or tactical superiority is, therefore, now constantly confronted with a particularly complex challenge to overcome. The nuclear issue posed by Iran is a more sophisticated example than Hezbollah's resilience, but basically it's the same trend. We can also see, despite U.S. and British opposition, that the rest of the world managed to impose (albeit painfully) the beginnings of responsibility for the destruction of the Lebanon's or Palestine's public and private infrastructure on Israel. The potential deterrent effect of the Israeli nuclear arsenal is thus indirectly questioned, because one wonders which world powers would support the near-destruction of the principal global oil installations and the sterilization of areas with huge concentrations of hydrocarbon reserves for decades (in case of a nuclear strike on Iran or another Persian Gulf power). There again, raw potential military power does not

---

[95] One can note that the Israeli army has been bureaucratized which means that its current senior officers have no practical combat experience, unlike previous generations who had. Its constant use in the Palestinian territories has only taught it methods of maintaining order while their training has been increasingly based on the U.S. model. The Israeli senior officers who planned the military failure of summer 2006 followed the same training as the senior U.S. officers who planned the current Iraqi quagmire. Incidentally, the political leaders also have a very similar intellectual make-up.

necessarily equal the actual political capacity. "Having the ability to do" and "actually doing" are two completely different things.

• **Uncertainty about the nature of long-term U.S. support for Israel**

The U.S. failures in the Middle East, especially the stalemate in Iraq, amid widespread weakening of the United States, are now feeding a questioning of the special relationship between Israel and the United States, fueled as much by opponents of unconditional U.S. support for Israel[96] as by the advocates of that same support, worried about Israel's inability to implement U.S. priorities in the region[97]. Depending on political and economic developments in the United States, Israel may even face a very sharp reversal of trends which could rock America's strategic choices in the Middle East. In the Unites States voices increasingly are being raised to denounce U.S. blind conformity regarding the Israeli-Palestinian conflict. The situation has already evolved from the loud unwavering support of the Bush team to the uncomfortable unwavering support of the Obama administration[98]. This combination of circumstances must not make U.S. forget that the United States was a country little inclined to support Israel until the 1960s.

• **The EU's growing and sustainable influence in the Middle East**

One can consider the fact that the Europeans are making a military return to the Middle East exactly 50 years after being ousted by the American-Soviet duo during the Suez crisis as pure hearsay. However, it is nonetheless true that 7,000 European soldiers now provide protection to the northern border of Israel and keep the Lebanese coastline under surveillance. This event has always been considered undesirable by successive Israeli governments and Washington in recent decades. Far from being a distribution of tasks desired by the U.S. administration or by the authorities in Tel Aviv, this is indeed the Europeans' great return to the area (happily with other objectives than those of the colonial and postcolonial period). This return is sustainable because it is accompanied by strongly favourable public opinion and that Europeans see the Lebanese operation as a first step towards a leading role in the settlement of the Israeli-Palestinian conflict. The growing European importance in the region will be accompanied by a much more balanced approach to the conflict and mark the end of the era of automatic support for Israel which has been the "American sponsorship" of the former peace process of the last decade. In this regard, the reality is that there is neither U.S. sponsorship, nor peace process. But it shows

---

[96] The famous article by Mearsheimer and Walt, published at Harvard in March 2006, illustrates this trend's rise. Source: John F. Kennedy School of Governance, http://ksgnotes1.harvard.edu/Research/wpaper.nsf/rwp/RWP06-011

[97] The recent article by Aron Raskas, entitled "What U.S. Jews now expect from Israel" is very enlightening on the subject. Aron Raskas is an eminent leader of several major Jewish organizations in the United States. Source: Haaretz, 04/09/2006

[98] Unlike Bush, he claims to be changing the situation, in fact. Criticism is growing in the United States on its inability to make anything move in the region.

the opposite of what underlies this assumption concerning the Europeans' role. The U.S. monopoly over current European leaders has completely blocked Europe's rising importance in the region. France in particular, which no longer has a foreign policy of its own since Nicolas Sarkozy came to power, has completely neutralized any European attempt at action in the region. If this assumption is valid as I believe it will, therefore, have to wait until the middle of the decade to contribute to the region's evolving situation.

• **The Israeli-Palestinian conflict becomes a real regional conflict**
This means that the conflict over the future of Israelis and Palestinians becomes a conflict that mainly involves the regional powers more and more and the non-regional powers less and less. This is also a logical consequence of the preceding limits. The disappearance of the USSR, lasting weakening of the United States and the rise in EU or Iranian power illustrates a phenomenon of "realignment". During the 1950-1990 decades, the major decisions regarding this conflict were taken in Moscow and Washington. From the beginning of the 1990s until summer 2006, it was in Washington. Now, and for a long time, it will be in an area bounded by Tehran to the East, Ankara to the North, Brussels to the West and Riyadh to the South that will decide the broad outline of the Israelis and Palestinians' future. This does not mean that the rest of world is of no importance, only of secondary importance.

Scenario A: The end of the state of Israel, towards single Jewish communities in a Muslim Middle East

Scenario A presumes, in particular, major political continuity from the 1995-2010 decade. Instead of incorporating new constraints weighing on its environment, the leaders and the people of Israel continue to rely on a rationale of a full-blooded power struggle with their neighbours (primarily the Palestinians) and the rest of the world (particularly by refusing to recognize UN resolutions that they do not like). Politically, it is especially the option of taking power by Benjamin Netanyahu and confidants. It also implies the failure of the revival of the process of Arab unity, paving the way for a growing religious influence (Islamic radicalization) of the entire Middle East. This trend would mark Iran's continuation as a regional power, including a satellization of a large part of Iraq as well as a domino-like collapse of pro-Western regimes[99] from Egypt to Morocco. Egypt is, in fact, now in a situation of "end of a reign" which positions the Muslim Brotherhood as the main force capable of taking power after President Mubarak[100].

---

[99] The West's impotence in preventing Iran's possession of nuclear weapons is a given. Israeli-American preventive action in the current context would only increase the likelihood of Scenario A happening.

[100] In this country there is an exhaustion of the dominant trends of recent decades. Initiated in the 70s when Egypt changed their allegiance from close to the USSR to the American sphere of influence, it especially enabled an Egyptian-Israeli peace playing a "buffer" role for Egypt regarding the extension of trends affecting the Middle East towards the Maghreb. But peace with Israel never embedded itself in Egyptian

Under these conditions, as far as the horizon of the decade 2010-2020, all Israel's direct and indirect neighbours (except the EU) will become fiercely hostile, all whilst having increased military strategic capacity. An open military conflict with several neighbouring countries with the direct involvement of Iran or other Gulf powers then becomes inevitable. For the reasons given already, except Israel suffering a direct nuclear attack first, it is likely that major world powers (members of the Security Council) will prevent the use of Israel's nuclear arsenal. The rise of tensions and the beginning of a conventional conflict, preceded by a hail of missiles falling on Israel, will first cause the rapid exodus of about one million Israeli citizens who also hold European or American passports[101], 20% of Israel's Jewish population. The European Union and the United States will accommodate them without difficulty, especially if they avoid a direct military engagement with totally unpredictable consequences.

Then military ground offensives, accompanied by the Israeli failure to stop the firing of missiles at the heart of the country (as the crisis of summer 2006 has already shown) will cause a rapid collapse of the country whose very small size mitigates against the creation of several long-term frontlines[102].

Thus, in the space of a few short weeks, the state of Israel will be gone[103]. On the other hand, three to four million ex-Israeli citizens of the Jewish faith will remain in the region; a priori the poorest or those whose families are from countries not wishing to give them shelter (probably like Russia, Ethiopia, etc.). For the International Community, the problem will take the form of a reversal of that, created in 1948, of Palestinian refugees. Probably one or two million of them will still find refuge in Europe, the United States, Canada, Australia or Latin America. But large Jewish communities will remain in the former Israel's territory which will become a new source of tension. So while the UN will seek to negotiate the best possible status for these communities, we will likely witness the emergence of Jewish terrorism, locally and internationally, claiming the re-establishment of the State of Israel.

---

public opinion and no credible player in the post-Mubarak era seems eager to rein in Egyptian public opinion on the matter.

[101] Especially with EU enlargement. Source: Jerusalem Centre for Public Affairs, Jewish Political Studies Review, 2005 and Autumn 2001

[102] During the 1967 War, it wouldn't have taken much for such a situation to happen. All distances in the region are measured in tens of kilometres and any significant breakthrough makes the reestablishment of a new front line very difficult.

[103] France, for example, experienced a sudden collapse of the whole of its state apparatus during the rapid penetration of German forces in June 1940. Such a situation is usually the product of a complex mix of irresponsibility of the elite, the people's unpreparedness and not taking new balances of power into account that make what is supposed to be "impossible", possible.

Scenario B: A lasting Israeli state, a partner with an Arab world in the process of regional integration

Scenario B assumes a major break with the policy pursued during the 1995-2010 decade. The Israeli leaders and people positively accommodate the new constraints on their environment and break with the rationale of a balance of power vis-à-vis their neighbours (primarily Palestinians) and the rest of the world (especially by beginning to recognize UN resolutions that they do not like).

Today, it is very difficult to identify the leaders or credible political force that can play such a role. Nevertheless it is present at the core of the young generation in Israel. This is the fourth generation, after that of the "founders" (extinct for twenty years or so), the "builders" (of which Sharon was the last political example) and that of the "heirs" (of which Olmert and Netanyahu are the most inspiring examples). What it will do is still uncertain, but some of these 20-35 year olds are trying to begin a new era, that of Israel's integration into its regional environment. This scenario B also assumes the success, albeit limited, of a process of Arab unity. After the eradication of pan-Arabism by the West, beginning with the '60s, and the consequential rise of pan-Islamism of which bin Laden is a successful product, today we are witnessing a return towards the hope of Arab unity among the young Arab elite.

This trend is particularly nourished by three complementary events. First, the feeling of humiliation generated by the U.S. invasion of Iraq and of helplessness in the face of the unilateral policy of Israel, second, the increasing visibility of the successful process of European unity which generates a real wish to copy it and, third, a growing concern that U.S. failures currently benefit non-Arab Muslim forces (Iran, Pakistan, etc.) especially, using Muslim religious identity at the expense of Arab identity. The revival of the process of unifying the Arab world would help to significantly reduce the feeling of inferiority and inequality, pervasive in Arab countries and now feeding a sense of injustice favourable to fundamentalists. The EU, because of its growing role in the region, will strengthen this trend and even the nature of its process of external relations will lead it to favour a process of Arab regional integration. The failure of Euro-Med process like that, from its birth, of the project for the Union for the Mediterranean ushered in by the French President Nicolas Sarkozy, makes it look for alternatives at any rate. This premise, over a period of 10 to 15 years, is not a figment of the imagination. It is rooted in trends, still fragile, but already at work now.

If these assumptions are confirmed, during the 2010-2020 decade, Israel will be able to substantially contribute to improving its own environment especially acting as a facilitator of this process of nascent Arab unification. Its location at the crossroads of several countries key for the success of such a process (Egypt, Lebanon, Iraq, Syria, etc.) offers it remarkable strategic advantages. Its ability, in such a context, to be the preferred vehicle of European or American partnerships with the rest of the Middle East, will further reinforce this situation. The paradox, in relation to the current dominant ideology in Tel Aviv and Washington, is that it is a unified and powerful Arab world would be much less problematic for Israel's existence than a fragmented Middle East in the throes of a war between Islam and Christianity, East and West, Arabs and Americans.

The Middle East will not remain outside the twenty-first century indefinitely. And a future Beirut-Cairo TGV fast train link, a technically possible project on the 2020 horizon would, in any event, have to go through Jerusalem or Tel Aviv. One of the crucial points of this development will be the renunciation by both Israel and the Palestinians (and other Arab peoples) to make Jerusalem a political capital. Whether single, double, triple or quadruple, Jerusalem must not become a political capital. It is by renouncing the symbol dear to the hearts of all parties that the way forward in Scenario B can come true. Inspired in particular by the experience of European construction, it is in effect one of the key messages the International Community must communicate. It will be a matter of "inhibiting power" to move the issues of confrontation to cooperation, instead of using it to try to crush the opposition.

Scenario B might seem to be very optimistic, but it is also inspired by history, especially the recent one of the European continent, or in countries like South Africa, where the worst seemed inevitable.

The Israeli-Lebanese crisis then the stalemate in Gaza has opened a door to a future that can give rise to these two scenarios. It is, of course, for the players directly concerned to define their responses based on these alternatives. But it is also for Europeans, a rising force in the region, to be aware of their heavy responsibilities.

Without radical change of course between now and 2014-2015, at the Israeli-Palestinian level, as well as the international one (including a comeback by Europeans in what is their immediate neighbourhood), the State of Israel is heading for a fall around 2020.

The Resurgence of Turkey
2010-2020, the gradual exit from the Western camp

Thanks to the ongoing systemic crisis and the rapid weakening of United States power and the Western framework on which this power rests, Turkey is fundamentally redefining its key geopolitical interests. The new priorities, in the process of early development, will constitute, between now and 2014, the deepest questioning conducted by Ankara since its NATO entry in 1952. This process illustrates a return to their antecedents, towards the Kemalist vision of Turkey's vital interests[104], that is to say, a break with the agenda set for Turkey by the dominant powers. It is ironic enough, moreover, that it should be the leaders of a religious.-inspired party, the AKP, which is initiating these changes. The geopolitical economic and trade consequences of this change in direction are significant because it challenges the traditional view of a Turkey that is pro-Western and awaiting EU integration.

As is often the case in the eastern Mediterranean region, it's the relationship with Israel which is a reliable indicator of the direction of relations of a country with the Western camp since, for over a decade, the Western camp is defined by a Washington/Tel Aviv line of command. However, in this area in recent months, Turkey has begun to deviate markedly from this ruling line which it was, on the contrary, required to constantly toe for many years. The violent attack in Gaza by the Israeli army in December 2008 was the event which marks the very clear beginning of this change, in tone first, then direction. In effect, since then Ankara has gradually begun to reverse back down the whole of the path built in recent years on the subject of cooperation with the Jewish state, both diplomatically and in military terms. The latest examples to date have been the decision to stop authorizing Israeli aircraft training in Turkish skies and the refusal to participate in NATO exercises in October 2009, with which Israel was involved, to announce joint manoeuvres with Syria[105] in the same breath. Here we are already very far from the military strategic behaviour expected from a faithful ally of the United States and a leading member of NATO.

However, this development on the regional geo-strategic plan has been in incubation since the downfall of the USSR, when the "cul-de-sac" in which Turkey found itself for the decades of the Cold War is back as a vast open space where the potential for cultural, economic and trade expansion is immense. Turkey under "orders" was already perceived as a country increasingly reluctant to have to dress up in Western uniform for regional targets increasingly alien to Turkish interests[106]. As long as there was the Cold War and the Soviet threat on its borders,

---

[104] Kemal Ataturk, founder of modern Turkey, had indeed both thought and wanted a Turkey which had broken with its Ottoman past and a Turkey rejecting the choices made for it by the dominant powers at the beginning of the twentieth century (the United Kingdom and France in particular). Its rejection of the Treaty of Sevres and its territorial consequences for Turkey is a prime example. In his will, he also clearly expressed what the conduit was that could link it to legitimate future heirs: "I leave, as a spiritual legacy, no verse, no dogma, no rule set in stone. My spiritual heritage is science and reason (...). Everything in this world is changing rapidly. The concept of happiness and sadness is changing, over time, among peoples and individuals. Noting, in this context, that one has known how to invent methods that are eternally valid which would be tantamount to denying the constant evolution of ideas and science. (...) Those who, after me, would wish to move forward in my wake, never departing from reason and science, will become my spiritual heirs". This would particularly include those having the courage to reject outdated customs.

[105] One certainly remembers the scandal caused by the Turkish President, Recep Erdogan at Davos in January 2009 when he abruptly left the stage because he wasn't given the same amount of time to speak as the Israeli President, Shimon Peres.

[106] As Washington's great difficulties to convince Ankara to let it use its bases in Turkey to attack Iraq in 2002/2003 have already hinted at.

Turkey willingly accepted being a "Western Knight" on the Middle Eastern chessboard. But, since 1989, the divergence of interests between the Knight and the King or Queen is increasing a little more strongly every year, which bodes ill for the sequel at two levels:

- First, Turkey will be increasingly less responsive to Washington's stimuli as evidenced by a growing series of negative reactions, causing a rise in hostile[107] tensions to Ankara even within the Alliance. One now sees something new: public questioning about Turkey's legitimacy within NATO, expressed by leaders of the Alliance's other member states.

- Secondly, the action of the Alliance and/or Washington in the region will be increasingly handicapped by a Turkey reluctant to obey and which, in contrast, develops its own strategic regional rationale possibly opposed to those of the Alliance. Ankara's good relationship with Tehran[108] is another glaring example. Here we are far from any idea of reinforced sanctions or effective embargo, however vigorously advocated by Washington.

In a nutshell, the relationship between Turkey and NATO is reaching a point of no return. The Turkish case only illustrates moreover the more general problem of a rapidly disintegrating Alliance, whose leader no longer has the vision or the means to supervise all the members.

Ironically, it is the other constituent of the "anchorage" of Turkey to the West, that's to say the promise of European Union accession, which is probably a decisive factor allowing this exit from the Western camp. It is, in effect, this untenable promise that was set in motion by the lack of courage and imagination of European leaders, via the formal opening of an accession process in 2005, which created the two major conditions for this new course of Turkish foreign policy:

- On the one hand, the democratic constraints of EU accession have increasingly forced the Turkish military to return to their barracks and stay there. For decades they were used to leading the country in the shadow of political puppets, dismissing them if necessary when the polls produced results that upset them. Posing as a guarantor of Ataturk's legacy, they especially benefited in controlling the country to make the most of the manna dropped by NATO, the EU and the United States, which compensated their loyalty to the Western camp[109]. Their weakness has thus deprived the West of

---

[107] Like in April 2009, when Turkey opposed to Fogh Rasmussen's NATO bid as new Secretary General because of his support to Danish media over the caricature crisis.

[108] The Turkish President, Recep Erdogan, insists the Iranian President Mahmoud Ahmadinejad qualifies as a friend of Turkey and states he doesn't accept the two burdens and two measures applied to Iran on nuclear issues

[109] The IMF has also played a significant role since Turkey has been one of its main beneficiaries for decades, allowing the West to run the country by proxy. The exiting of an IMF adjustment programme in 2008 also

one of its most faithful allies at the heart of Turkish society. Another example of the irony of history.

- On the other hand, the obvious reluctance of the EU, and particularly the vast majority of public opinion[110], faced with the prospect, however remote, of an enlargement to Turkey has been clear to Turkish citizens for four years. At the same time, the sudden discovery that the so-called "accession negotiations"[111] were not real negotiations but, on the contrary, a very real obligation on Turkey's part to fully adopt 90,000 pages of EU moral, commercial, economic and cultural legislation (only the timing of the "EU acquis" is in fact negotiable), triggered a popular feeling of rejection in the face of what was seen as a "colonialism by legislation". In Turks less than forty years old, the belief has thus gradually emerged that Europeans didn't want them and that their country had reached deadlock. This awareness was a fundamental event since it ended four decades of unchallenged domination of a formal discussion for making entry into Europe the only desirable future for the country. And simultaneously it has brought the Muslim party in power, who had only joined the EU adhesion project[112] under duress, a new wave of opinion, non religious., but now opposed (or at least hesitant) to EU accession process.

From Russia, whose citizens fall over each other on the Turkish beaches, to Central Asia where Ankara is pursuing a dynamic cultural and commercial policy towards the Turkish-speaking countries, through Iran and Syria, Turkey is developing, at high speed, a new diplomacy that attempts to join the politico-historical area of the Ottoman heritage, Muslim religious proximity, its own interests as a regional power and its status as a preferred crossing point. Everything is played via the pendulum effect, where NATO and the EU are increasingly elements of Ankara's diplomatic game, and no longer a fundamental element (as was the case for NATO) or central objective (as was the case for the EU).

So that Americans and Europeans do not misunderstand, there will be no turning back. NATO being, in any event, in the process of disintegration, there is no reason for Ankara not to continue its lone ride towards an intermediate position in the centre of a geopolitical balance comprising Russia, the EU, the Iran and any

---

matches the beginning of the most visible period of the new course of Turkish diplomacy. Incidentally Ankara is now very reluctant to take IMF loans once more.

[110] Now an increasing proportion of European elite no longer wishes Turkish entry into the EU. Recent diplomatic developments in Turkey have convinced them that, from now on, Ankara has a vision of the future less and less compatible with the common project.

[111] For decades, the Turkish elite, not denied by their European counterparts, had allowed Turkish citizens to believe that Turkish accession to the EU would be a process where each party would, after a fashion, meet halfway. From 2005 this lie began to shatter.

[112] Indeed, traditionally, the pro-Islamic movement in Turkey was opposed to EU entry. But if Paris was well worth a mass, Ankara is well worth a hypothetical enlargement.

influential power between its southern borders and Egypt (Washington at present). NATO's last loyal allies are the Turkish army's current generals. Ten years hence, around 2020, they will have been replaced by rising generations[113] who more than those previously are identifying the future of their country with this myth of the "bridge between East and West". And a bridge belonging to one of the banks to which it connects is no longer a bridge but a cul-de-sac[114].

This applies equally to the European Union. With token bureaucracy, Brussels and Ankara will continue the accession negotiations, even if the political will is no longer there. But they will not succeed and will stall year after year in general indifference. Because any extension is always the result of a political will, and only a political will.

However, the main sponsor of this expansion, namely Washington, now has plenty of other fish to fry and no longer has the influence to overcome the strong opposition of European public opinion (it can't even keep European troops in Afghanistan). And in the EU, no leader can get on his soapbox over Turkey's entry and risk losing the elections.

In Ankara, a different future to that of a European Turkey is taking hold. If the EU realizes that soon enough and offers Turkey a high level of strategic partnership, this dream will be one of a Turkish Turkey, an intermediary between the different axes that surround it. If Brussels is locked into its accession project, without any alternative, it takes the risk of pushing Ankara into a conflicting dream, that of a Muslim Turkey. Let's not forget the irony of history that often wishes one to get the result which is diametrically opposed to that which one is looking for if one forgets to take the dream into account: the expectations of the people with whom one is dealing.

In conclusion, far from it being worrying for Europe, Turkey's evolution outside the Western camp, which is itself in full decay, is a facet of the global systemic crisis, and the progressive erasure of the structures inherited by the world after 1945, which can enable Europeans between now and 2015 to have an appeased Turkey as a partner, able to be an effective intermediary with the entire Middle East and Central Asia.

And from 2014 Turkey, because of the Balkans, will be driven to begin publicly redefining its relationship with the EU.

---

[113] The only risk remaining, for the next five years, that an attempted military coup launched by retiring generals backed by Washington. But the probability is very low and it probably would end like that of the Russian generals against Mikhail Gorbachev in 1991.

[114] Moreover, Turkey is a dual bridge, between East and West, but also between the banks of the Black Sea and the Mediterranean. Without forgetting, that in the twenty-first century, a bridge is also (especially) an oil or gas pipeline, two areas where Turkey is centrally positioned with the Nabucco project, to which Iran is the key.

The Balkans 2014, the last EU enlargement

In effect, the saga of the EU's enlargements will reach its conclusion in the middle of this decade. Indeed, the combination of a growing European public opinion in opposition to enlargement and the lasting weakening of the United States/United Kingdom duo, the main force supporting the dilution of the EU into a vast zone of free trade and Atlantic security, guarantees that we are reaching the end of this European expansion in successive waves. And the epilogue will probably take place at Sarajevo in July 2014 with a solemn declaration of the EU integration of the entire Balkans before 2020.

The opportunity to end a century of European civil wars by integrating the Balkans into the EU is compelling in symbolic terms as well as in terms of political necessity. To be very clear, I am convinced that enlargement to the Balkans will mark the end of any further EU enlargement[115] for many decades. It is worthwhile, therefore, dwelling a little on the Balkan case.

In effect, if there is an expansion which directly corresponds with the original purpose of the process of European integration begun after the Second World War and whose objective was to prevent further European wars, it is certainly the enlargement to the Balkans. And to leave the Balkans out of the EU for longer than the next ten years is a serious. strategic error because it will again become, right in the heart of Europe, the fixation point of powers in competition with the EU like Turkey[116], Russia and the United States by offering them remarkable leverage for destabilizing Europe (for those who so wish).

On July 28, 2014, in Sarajevo, the European Union and Balkan countries have, therefore, a unique opportunity to conclude what remains an unfinished work, the end of European civil wars. In effect, it is in this very city that the deadly spiral of twentieth century European wars was set in motion on July 28, 1914. Because History doesn't give an opportunity twice, a growing number of political forces and European leaders are beginning to push this symbolic date onto the EU agenda.

Of course, like any powerful symbol, two trends are already clashing with the issue of EU democratization as a backcloth. Some political forces[117] want this date to be used to organize, at the time of the June 2014 European elections, the first trans-European referendum on enlargement, namely the Balkans. While the bulk of

---

[115] Except Norway and Switzerland which will gradually join the EU over the coming years. Norway, when its oil reserves are nearly exhausted. Switzerland when its banks are in a similar state, that is to say soon given the major setbacks for Swiss bank secrecy since the crisis began.

[116] From Bosnia-Herzegovina to Kosovo and Albania, Muslim Turkey which (re) takes shape will find very active intermediaries. Russia will fully play its Slavic solidarity especially with Serbia. And the United States has already turned Albania into a "U.S. aircraft carrier" which must be unravelled.

[117] Including Newropeans, the European political movement that I chair.

the EU wants to do what it usually does, without any democratic control, with only a televised fancy celebration for European spectators and not citizens. Anyway, July 2014 can be an historic moment for enlargement because the reasons that makes it possible the enlargement to the Balkans fully illustrate why the other enlargements under consideration will not be feasible politically in the foreseeable future (at least twenty years).

Of course, the road to Sarajevo 2014 is littered with obstacles.

The first of these is the total lack of EU political ambition in relation to the Balkans, *which directly threatens the ability of the younger generation to exit this region from its violent past. In effect, without a clear message that they share the same fate as the rest of European youth, they will be unable to successfully resist nationalist leaders and parties.* The only thing the EU should have done so far is show that it can replace NATO militarily to keep the very unstable peace in the region. Sending troops, consultants and money is not a long term policy. Although it seems that the EU's intention is to continue on this path forever, at least when one looks at its shortage of long-term projects for the Balkans.

However, it is actually possible to "sell" this enlargement to the Balkans and EU public opinion. In effect, contrary to the view of most EU politicians and institutions, it is possible to "sell" Balkan accession to the EU to the majority of European citizens because the region represents the only argument that can still convince voters to support this new enlargement. European public opinion doesn't have a clearly established position on this issue. Contrary to that on Turkey or the Ukraine, in effect no coherent and organized opposition exists to the accession of the Balkan countries. So anything is possible. And, an important advantage, the reasons for Balkans integration are easy to understand. Essentially, there are two main arguments.

On the one hand, the Balkans is already a major problem for the EU and will remain so in the future. Therefore the only question for the EU is whether it wants to manage the Balkan problem internally or externally. On the other hand, Balkan accession does not alter the internal or external strategic balance of the EU. These countries are already within European borders and their total population has shrunk (about 25 million people). It's not like the Ukraine or Turkey, whose accession would profoundly alter the EU's internal balance (because of the newcomers' demographic impact) and its relations with its geopolitical environment (by moving the EU boundaries towards Asia and the Middle East).

Therefore, the EU only has two choices:

- Either it continues as it is now, that is to say by choosing no clear option, talking of a possible accession but only on an individual basis with each state, with no clear deadline or procedure while continuing to act according to the status quo inherited from Dayton. In doing so, it would prevent all the

87

forces that wish to establish viable democracies and peaceful relations in the region from gaining power because it would be up to the current nationalist forces (often anti-democratic as well) to preserve the fragile peace. In short, to preserve peace in the short term, it must support the forces that are against the goals of peace and democracy for the region over the long term.

- Or the EU chooses to put in place a clear policy essentially saying three things. The EU deals with the region as a whole. Each country will have its own objectives, each country will also depend on its neighbours' achievements. We must learn European solidarity from the beginning of the accession process, particularly in this region. And we all know that enlargements are ultimately a political issue, mainly managed as "big bangs" as was the case during the most recent ones. The EU establishes a clear agenda with a symbolic date, July 28, 2014, and a symbolic place where the accession ceremony will be held for all countries concerned: Sarajevo. The EU pledges to make every effort to convince its citizens to accept the Balkans in its centre at that time and binds it to a referendum on the accession of Balkan countries during the European elections in 2014.

The Balkan countries have no realistic alternative to joining the EU on their side. And despite the rhetoric, they well know it. This is another aspect that differentiates the enlargement to the Balkans from other enlargement projects such as Turkey or the Ukraine. Turkey has another choice which is clearly more and more attractive to it as it was discussed in the chapter devoted to it. As for the Ukraine, its geographical and ethnic composition makes for, at least, a separation of the country into two, on each side of the Dnieper, leaving the Western part to get closer to the EU, while the Eastern part would once again incorporate itself with Russia, it has no choice but to remain a buffer state between the EU and Russia. Moreover, in ten years it can become a gangway between these two large entities. The pace of the weakening of U.S. presence in the region will directly determine the ability of Kiev to be a factor of reconciliation or division between the EU and Russia.

Adapt France to the "world after"
Ten years to exit the two century-old centralized model

Before examining the possible course of events for France and the French in the coming decade, in the face of the global crisis and the turmoil it causes, we must understand the situation France is entering this decade. If there really is a global crisis, there is also a serious. crisis, not of French identity[118], but with the country's elite who have been unable, for almost 20 years, to propose a both exciting and realistic vision to their 65 million fellow citizens.

This leads to a specific recommendation to help the French, and indirectly the Europeans therefore, to face the challenges of the world after the crisis. They have "ten years to break Paris". It's not a case of destroying a city that I love enormously. But it's to get France out of the setting of the last two centuries, this setting which is truly in the course of exploding worldwide under the effect of the crisis. So that five hundred million Europeans, and sixty five million French people at their core, can get to play a comparable game with the Chinese, Indians, Russians or Americans, it's going to have to reinvent itself according to the new world game which materializes and which has been broadly described in the first part of this book. To equally avoid a "takeover" of Paris, as took place with the Americanists in the middle of the last decade, it is essential to end this centralized pyramid model which allows any major power (and the world will now be full of powers much larger than France) to easily take control of the main levers of power in the country.

Polycentrism, which is also one of the ways forward for the EU institutional structure on the 2020[119] horizon, is a natural choice to maintain a unified state while increasing the pillars on which it rests. We must not only diversify the recruitment of elites[120], but also and especially their education and intellectual and cultural environment. And it's a task that doesn't stop with the end of one's studies. The wealth of France is its diversity. The weakness of France is its elite's lack of diversity which thus makes them very susceptible to the first intellectual virus that shows up.

The network of high speed trains is itself a map of likely homes for state institutions: Lyon, Marseille, Bordeaux, Toulouse, Lille, Strasbourg, etc. are intended to accommodate large state institutions: Court of Auditors, Constitutional Council, Ministries, etc. Even Parliament could effectively move, for example to

---

[118]And here it's not a matter of the debate launched by Nicolas Sarkozy's team or in fact it is, but rather conversely. I learned through my activities in Europe, where the question of European identity comes up regularly (it's a classic deadly boring debate sponsored by Brussels) that when a group discusses its identity, it doesn't know where it's going any more. And so it tries, in vain, to look in the past, for a reply that can only be in the future. One is always what one will be, never what one was. But obviously, when the leaders of a group haven't either any idea about the future, or an idea they do not want to reveal because it is contrary to the interests of the group, then they make identity a key issue, a prerequisite for any new big decision. Meanwhile, people run in circles, in meaningless debates because they are looking where they can't find an answer: yesterday.

[119] This is a development that I detail later in this book.

[120] Not by charity, as the current government advocates by the example of Sciences-Po.

Lyon, once the capital of Gaul and much more central than Paris[121]. Germany works like that, and its State, whilst federal[122], is much more efficient than the French one in many and not insignificant ways, its press is richer, more democratic, more widely dispersed geographically. Thus there are regional elites that provide a truly varied sustenance to the national elite. This prevents the easy takeover of the levers of power by the installation of a small local coterie as was the case in Paris. In fact, Paris has to suffer the same fate as Brussels which, to allow the EU to become a truly democratic and genuine power, must also be "broken" as well as its European institutions spread across several European capitals, as analysed further. Moreover, in such a context, Paris could be a serious candidate to host the European executive during the 2020 decade. But there again, France must no longer be summarized as Paris!

To finish with the features of this essential complete overhaul of France's administrative and political governance system, it only remains to say that the only way to reduce the French state's now unsupportable inefficiency is by addressing the real source of its unnecessary excess costs, namely its Parisian "head". The main cause of the country's budgetary waste is in the ministries' central services, at the head of these overstaffed hierarchies that populate the capital's central districts. It is not the country post office and postman that are expensive, nor the simple soldier or college teacher. What costs a fortune and which very often serves no purpose is the multitude of managers, general managers, advisers and other inspectors of all kinds who have a string of wages, allowances, bonuses and other benefits of office without bringing any added value whatsoever to the national community. They serve especially as sinecures and golden resting places for the different clans of Parisian powers. Radical reform can only take place by setting an example, that requires the most powerful, the senior hierarchy to first of all apply to themselves the rules to which they want to subject others.

It's not even anything to do with democracy, it's a matter of managing human groups and effectiveness of collective action. The servants of the national interest, and there are many in the administration, know that well. However the current Parisian elite do exactly the opposite, daily displaying a counter-example of their addresses on effectiveness and individual effort to serve the collective interest. There isn't even a need to give examples anymore because there are so many. Yet, for an effective State, we have an urgent need to successfully confront the challenges of "the world after" which will, in particular, require the Civil Service

---

[121] Again the requirements of the coming decade and century are the exact reverse of the actions of the current Parisian elite who are attempting to overturn the modest decentralization process undertaken more than twenty years ago. Like any mercenary elite, or without real legitimacy, they seek to control instead of stimulating.

[122] And in the French case I'm speaking about, it's not a question of creating a federal state. Polycentrism is a unified state resting on several bases, instead of a pyramid centralism which we have had for more than two centuries.

to be reactive, able to build trans-European public service networks to bring Europe and the common good together and even to adapt themselves to international conditions by a rapid change. This example will have to come from above to change the State machine.

The change towards polycentrism[123] and the implementation of reforms at the very top of the hierarchical pyramids before anything else will have to be the two dominant trends or severe consequences will lead France towards the tragic scenario of the coming decades:

- Slow State decline towards third-world status, riddled with nepotism, corruption, subservience to powerful interests (private and/or foreign), the inability to systematically protect its territory.

- In the favourable setting offered by the European Union, triggering a wave of questioning in France (as is already the case in Italy, Spain, Belgium or the United Kingdom) on the territorial integrity of the country (global geopolitical dislocation will essentially take this form in Europe in its territorial aspect): increased agreements over border regions with their German, Spanish and Italian twins challenging Parisian control, resurgence of Corsican, Basque and Breton separatist terrorism, etc. Paris mustn't believe that God gave it France. What history has done, history can undo. The shape of our "eternal France" is in fact only two hundred years old, that's to say, the historical period which the world is in the course of leaving. France will not come out of it the way we knew it.

Already border areas and towns from Strasbourg to Nice, benefitting from the removal of borders related to European integration and responding to the weakening of French central power (growing transfer of costs and responsibilities to local authorities, increasingly heavy reductions in the local presence of the State's machinery such as justice, the army, etc.), are multiplying partnerships with their neighbours of other member states, turning their backs on Paris as soon as they can in terms of education, economic development, transport, etc. Every day the EU gives them more opportunities not to go via the capital to act at the core of the five hundred million Europeans market. The continuation of the strange situation that sees almost all the regions vote the opposite to Paris may be interpreted as a simple problem of "left against right", or as the emergence of a genuine « the French versus Paris » dilemma, especially if this trend continues once there has been a change in power in Paris.

In my view, there are really only two main options in fact, either its people and leaders prepare and organize its transformation so that being French twenty or thirty years from now should still be of value in the historical sense, or the French

---

[123] The organization in a network is the dominant fashion of our century, institutional polycentrism is the "State" version.

become both players and victims in a new violent upheaval to which they are accustomed to adapt to the world after the crisis and from which it is far from certain that France would exit unscathed

The choice offered by history for the next decade is, therefore, of equally strategic importance for France, not only for the world's large geopolitical groups.

To conclude this overview of the global next decade, if we add the impact of the dislocation phase on Russia and China, it will be very interesting to know whether this global systemic crisis will see the new EU style model of regional integration survive, or enforce the imperial model like the U.S., China and Russia. Depending on the factors identified above, this global systemic crisis could well be the last manifestation of crises that, for a hundred years, have succeeded in bringing down empires one after the other. A simple matter of adaptation to the socio-economic environment of the coming century.

Europe, a crucial decade
to anchor in the reality of the Europeans
and the world after the crisis

The project of European integration (Europe as it is routinely called) is also directly affected by the crisis. The decade which has just begun will play a decisive historical trial role in knowing whether the continent's integration process, initiated 60 years ago, will really enable Europeans to continue to influence the world's progress. But for Europeans, unlike Americans for example, this adaptation to the world after the crisis has already been underway for the last twenty years because it's not just Russia that has experienced the change in the world order since 1989 and the fall of the Berlin Wall. The EU also started its march towards the world of the twenty-first century from that moment.

European integration
A laboratory prototype suddenly cast into history in 1989

With the process of German reunification and, in fact Europe itself, which began in 1990, the clever makeshift job devised in the 50s and 60s by the founding generation of the Community project (Monnet, Schuman, de Gasperi, Adenauer, de Gaulle[124], etc.) was abruptly cast into history with a capital « H ». Until 1989, the European Community was in fact only a political item in the laboratory, quietly developed by a part of a continent, historically stagnant after 1945. Sheltered by the U.S. nuclear umbrella and protected from the Easterly winds by the Iron Curtain, the West Europeans had invented a new post-national political entity. But its construction in an artificial environment proved nothing about its viability in the real world. Hitherto it built up its rhythm, giving deadlines, meeting them or not, without any great consequence because, in fact, it existed in a virtual historical environment. The Federal Republic of Germany and its provincial capital, Bonn, was a perfect example.

The fall of the Berlin Wall suddenly shattered the laboratory walls and the prototype was suddenly faced with the harsh and unpredictable realities of history: German unification, stabilization of Eastern Europe, collapse of the Soviet Union, enlargements. The creation of the Euro was at the heart of the answers given by the leaders of the time (Mitterrand, Kohl, Gonzalez, Martens, Lubbers) so as to begin to anchor the European project in historical reality. For better or worse, by giving a single currency to the continent's major nations, it forced them to all sail together[125]. The global crisis has shown the relevance of this decision since the

---

[124] Whatever one may say, de Gaulle was also an architect of this process because he never sought to take France out of the Common Market and, on the contrary, tried to preserve its unifying coherence by preventing United Kingdom membership for as long as possible.

[125] Greece has also suffered the painful experience of the common discipline as its elite believed they could climb into the Euro boat and continue to enjoy the benefits of European integration without the drawbacks, as they had done with the European Union since 1982.

Eurozone has become one of the main centres of global stability and unquestionably one of the three major players in the global monetary system with the United States and China.

But the generation of decision makers that followed those who can be called the "last generation that experienced the war" (and therefore knew why they made Europe) did not know how to enhance the work of their predecessors. The Euro was an instrument bringing people much closer together and thus implying a further step to greater political integration. However, the rising importance of the "baby boom" generation for whom Europe has never been a rousing topic nor even a subject for thought, gradually led the EU's political direction into an impasse absent a vision of the future and therefore the lack of political will.

Since the mid-1990s, the European elite haven't known what to do with Europe except preventing its citizens taking control

I had the habit of saying that the generation of Mitterrand and Kohl whom I knew personally, especially during the intense lobbying to have Erasmus adopted in 1986-1987, found an instrument called "Europe" on their desk that they knew how to use to solve current problems every day. Whilst the political generation that followed them, and which will dominate until the middle of this decade, found a problem called "Europe" on their desk which they do not know what to do with each day. This attitude has led to what I consider to be "the lost decade" of 1999-2009, from the fall of the Santer Commission to the unpopular (and therefore counter-productive[126]) ratification of the Treaty of Lisbon.

Far from continuing the unifying drive of the continent's people that the adoption of the Euro and enlargement (and German unification) entailed and which meant an accelerated EU democratization in order to move the European project closer to its five hundred million citizens, the community elite locked themselves in a pyramidal-model, convinced that from the top of the European institutional pyramid, they would be able to face history and channel public opinion.

Here we find the same centralist disorder and increasingly divorced from reality, which affects the Parisian elite and the « French model ». This isn't surprising because the entire Community administrative machinery was based on the French model of the 1950s. To the same causes correspond the same effects,

---

[126] Counter-productive because one of the challenges posed by the transition towards the world after the crisis precisely consists of establishing the European project in the hearts of the people instead of trying to bypass them as the community elite did with this Treaty.

effects described in the previous chapter dealing with the problem of France and its elite in the face of the next decade's developments.

This wrong belief explains the unbroken series of failures achieved by this generation of leaders when it comes to European affairs, illustrated by several memorable examples:

- The collective resignation of the entire Santer Commission amid accusations of endemic fraud in the Brussels executive knowing that Brussels has made no significant changes as a result of this institutional shock: the bureaucrats who run the Commission, virtually for life[127], played a little game of musical chairs before a European Parliament which has no real power[128]; they made the Commissioners resign (unlike a democracy where the fuses are the civil servants) and everything continued as before, no Eurocrat has been troubled over all these cases of corruption or fraud.

- The "Mad Cow" crisis ended by convincing Europeans that the collective interest of five hundred million Europeans was the least of the worries of the Community administrative machine (of which Brussels is only the cherry on the cake composed of twenty-seven national bureaucracies).

- The predictable failure[129] of the draft European Constitution has dispersed what remained of any democratic conscience among the European elite. In France, the collusion between Americanists and Eurotechnos was really sealed at that time. Both groups agreeing that the people should be distanced from the important decisions. And elsewhere in Europe, the dangerous belief that people are too stupid to understand the major European issues take hold in the mediocre minds of the elite who don't know what to do with Europe other than profit from it themselves. By way of an anecdote, I have often reminded Eurocrats that when one is not paid by the EU, and hasn't the opportunity to attend regular working meetings in Rome, Paris, Berlin, Vienna, etc., the value of the European project quite legitimately demands some serious explaining. And if those who are paid by Europe and who can

---

[127] And enjoying judicial immunity incomparable with any other international institution

[128] From October 2004 I had alerted (in vain) the Governments concerned that the French and Dutch referenda would run straight into a brick wall if the democratic issue wasn't at least addressed in the campaign (in the absence of it appearing in the draft Constitution) and if the publicity machine didn't quickly stop repeating interminable images of balloons, children and the war between the French and Germans. New generations would arrive on the "European political market" that would no longer want to be treated like children on European affairs and who wouldn't have nightmares every night about the next Franco-German War.

[129] From October 2004 I had alerted (in vain) the Governments concerned that the French and Dutch referenda would run straight into a brick wall if the democratic issue wasn't at least addressed in the campaign (in the absence of it appearing in the draft Constitution) and if the publicity machine didn't quickly stop repeating interminable images of balloons, children and the war between the French and Germans. New generations would arrive on the "European political market" that would no longer want to be treated like children on Europeean affairs and who wouldn't have nightmares every night about the next Franco-German War.

professionally appreciate its diversity are not prepared to provide explanations, then they are elite in name only and it would be better to change profession. Moreover, the quality of democratic debate which preceded the referenda in France and the Netherlands, in contrast to the democratic void which precede the European elections, has clearly proved that there were very high popular expectations in terms of European debate... provided that there should be clear issues and that the elite are ready to assume their role of discussion enlighteners. Sadly, we're a long way from that.

- The repeated attempts of the Community system, clearly acting as an instrument of Washington and major European businesses, to pursue enlargement towards Turkey in particular, despite almost universal opposition in public opinion which detected a conversion of the European project into a specific case of economic and trade "regional-globalization".

- The shameful political contortions that allowed the French and Dutch leaders not to ask for the opinion of their people again on the Lisbon Treaty, which is only a slightly modified constitution, ended the "lost-decade"[130] with a manoeuvre that has distanced people even further from the Community institutional system.

The EU in the face of the challenge of its historical anchor in the people

This is the terrible result of these ten wasted years. Whilst it was necessary to strengthen the European project's popular support, of which the Euro, a legacy of the previous generation, provided the catalyst, the European elite have succeeded in the dramatic feat of alienating even more popular support for the EU system. Nevertheless I emphasize the distinction between European project and EU system because it is crucial for hoping that Europe should make a success of the decade which is beginning. There is a vast majority of Europeans convinced of the importance of the European integration project[131], but they are equally a majority to reject the EU system, the politico-administrative machine governing the EU. And these last ten years have greatly contributed to augment the number of these dissidents.

The EU's democratic window of opportunity in the coming decade lies exactly between these two widely shared beliefs. This is called EU democratization, that's to say, its institutional system's radical adaptation to an unprecedented democratic

---

[130] And this book is especially intended to be a contribution to avoid losing a second decade, which risks being the last for democracy and Europe.

[131] Looking back over the last twenty five years, I can even say that there has never been as many. Even the "nationalist" political forces are now compelled to position themselves in a European context as demonstrated by Libertas' challenge in the 2009 European elections.

reality: run a modern democracy, therefore complex, with five hundred million citizens from twenty-seven different countries, cultures and languages. The languages in the geographical structure of the institutional system, requires a radical examination of the evidence on which the present-day European Union rests. These points are expanded upon in specific chapters.

To illustrate the urgency of the challenge, let's remember that we do not drive a car with the same tools and methods that were used to build it. The EU's construction period has ended, we have entered its phase of governance and it is therefore necessary to review in full the basis on which it was founded almost sixty[132] years ago.

The Brussels elite are just as parochial as their Parisian counterparts

But to be fair, if the EU system's unpopular drift owes much to its French model, which faces the same problems nationally, it has also been aggravated at European level by corruption of the goals and methods orchestrated by Great Britain since Margaret Thatcher's time. The growing British influence in Brussels, sponsored by the U.S., has largely contributed to render a growing part of the Commission's action meaningless, moving it from a mission administration to a management bureaucracy without the means to carry out one or the other. Recruitment has continued with very generous base salaries, inherited from the days when nobody wanted to work for Europe, except a few idealistic missionaries, and when it was necessary to "go all out" to attract the necessary expertise, even when the examinations turned into competitions attracting tens of thousands of candidates, primarily motivated by the salaries.

Under these conditions, exit the mission due to the lack of missionaries. But at the same time, recruitment continued on the outdated basis of lawyers and economists whilst the Commission became a huge budget managing machine from where the increasing problems of management and the rising importance of fraud emanated. The States taking advantage of it, the post-1999 reforms not dealing with it, the last generation of "believers" therefore left the Commission at the beginning of the 2000s, leaving a machine going nowhere, unpopular and notionally run by the Commissioners with doubtful skills and effectively in the hands of senior management who for decades have lived in this common aquarium that Brussels had become.

---

[132] Several players from the generation of the European project's founders whom I knew, like Jean Guyot (first Financial Officer of the ECSC), Emnanuele Gazzo (founder of Agence Europe) or Henri Brugmans (founder of Bruges College of Europe) told me that what they had created was intended to be redone regularly to adapt to the changing world.

The most amazing is that "such a small world"[133] is convinced that it is very diverse and whilst it is made up of civil servants and experts (who are often people hoping to become civil servants themselves) there is nothing more similar than the thought patterns of two civil servants whatever their country of origin. In the style of the Parisian elite who are now composed solely of clones, the EU elite are of an astonishing intellectual consistency when one thinks they are supposed to understand and represent the diversity of twenty-seven countries. No wonder France as Paris and Europe as Brussels have increasing problems with their elite.

But the Eurocrats enjoy a relative excuse nevertheless. The absence of political leaders of stature for one decade now has condemned European officials to take the leading role, whilst in a democracy they are supposed to be only servants. It was necessary to run the machine, which they have done, without imagination, without revitalization, without daring. But that's precisely because they were thus that they were recruited as civil servants. One can't blame them.

The Eurozone, the only engine of European integration

Fortunately there was, nevertheless, a real institutional step forward in this lost decade, it's the slow emergence (often too slow) of the Eurozone as an engine of European integration. A natural consequence of the Euro's creation and the common destiny that it brings to those who share it, the Eurozone has helped to refocus the Community project on the continent, by marginalizing the United Kingdom, which doesn't share the continent's objectives at all (for another decade at least). The current crisis has greatly accelerated this marginalization and has even contributed to reversing the process. It is now the continent and the Eurozone, which weighs more and more on London, the City and their progress. This aspect will accelerate in the coming ten years since losing U.S. support and the City's power at the same time, the United Kingdom will find itself very weak and isolated.

In any case, it's the opportunity to recapture a part of the European project where it began to be badly diverted in the late 1980s, when the teams encouraged by Margaret Thatcher were all operational. The European Central Bank[134] has thus become the mainstay of European independence and the resumption of the project for continental integration. Therefore, it's really around the Eurozone that European political construction must be relaunched. The two components will be economic governance and its democratic control. It is by this means that the

---

[133] A world I know well, having worked in Brussels and Luxembourg in the 1990s.

[134] Which represents the future of the European institutional system not only because it has exited the archaic trinity of Brussels-Luxembourg-Strasbourg, but also its method of recruitment bans careers and immunity for life like the traditional EU system.

historic challenge of democratizing[135] the European project can be raised again, not by approaching it head-on via the twenty seven member-states.

Through the Euro, now a major international currency, the link is made quite naturally with Europe's other great challenge for the 2010-2010 decade, Europe's role in the world. As indicated earlier, the crisis represents a unique historical opportunity for Europeans to reposition themselves as one of the major forces shaping the coming century. We've already reviewed the advantages of Europe here, and it is certainly in targeting the international monetary system's imperative reconstruction that this role will evolve. Then, towards the middle of the decade, due to U.S. withdrawal from Europe and rising risks (more or less serious depending on the scenario), it will be time to merge the United Kingdom with a true leap ahead in joint defence. Until then, the joint diplomatic service, a useful development from the Lisbon Treaty, will have started to generate "the joint diplomatic interest"[136] on a daily basis, whatever the worth of the High Representative who is supposed to lead. After the middle of the decade, it will be necessary, of course, to move up a gear to take on the European role in the world if we want to avoid the world taking the tragic path to the following decade.

Solutions still exist for Europeans to succeed in playing this key role thus avoiding the tragic path to the world after the crisis. Beyond the monetary and geopolitical aspects already discussed, I have chosen to illustrate the challenges facing Europe in the decade ahead with six examples, demonstrating both the need to be innovative and describing the extent of the upheavals that lie ahead:

- The first two are advice to Europeans and their children concerning, first, the major changes ahead for the value of international credentials, and secondly, the foreign languages spoken by Europeans in 2020.

- Then, midway between citizens and institutions, I address the topic of the innovations needed for European policy of higher education post-Erasmus and, after a fashion, the issue of Islam's integration in Europe.

- Finally, destined for the political forces and European institutions, I am opening two key debates for the EU's democratization and its ability to adapt to the world after the crisis, namely, the new conditions that European construction places on progressive political forces and the geographic organization of European power, which is the political issue "par excellence".

---

[135] A process that can only come from below, from citizens and which has been in continuous development since the early 1990s: increasing power from the Erasmus generations, internet development and related lowering of the costs of organizational development on a European scale, collapse of the national political classes' credibility, widespread perception of the growing importance of European decisions. On this last point, the crisis has done a great service for the Eurozone.

[136] This is where the institutions are unbeatable, they automatically create their own raison d'être.

All six challenges are concerned with the way Europe can valorise its only real resource, its men and women.

R (evolution) in key foreign languages within the EU between now and 2020. French, German and Russian, the coming decade's winning threesome

The importance of an international language is directly related to the influence of the countries where it is spoken as the mother tongue. The "world after" the crisis will therefore experience a significant change regarding the hierarchy of international languages. First, globally, Chinese as well as Arabic will increasingly establish themselves as languages which are considered essential. The recent decisions of ICANN, the Internet' governing body, allowing the creation of domain names in other than Western alphabets, is proof. Now Chinese, Arabs, Japanese, Russians and others can create Internet addresses in their own alphabets, another sign of the end of an era of Western hegemony. Secondly, in Europe, the cumulative effects of European integration, the fading memory of the Second World War, the fall of the Iron Curtain and the rapid weakening of Anglo-Saxon influence is prompting sweeping changes in the linguistic landscape. Indeed, for rising generations in Europe, those who are less than twenty years old in 2010, the preferred languages for professional matters will undoubtedly be French and German and probably Russian as well. International Pidgin English placing itself as a basic communication tool, just able to get along will be insufficient to meet the increased communication requirements arising from European integration.

On this subject, one sees how much the comment on the future affects the immediate issues for every single one of us, because here it's a matter of the choices to make today for our own children. The individual and collective strategies on language education are in fact long-term processes requiring fundamental choices to be made nearly a generation in advance. Anticipation errors in this field will pay heavily offset by a total gap at a later date between linguistic supply and demand, between socio-economic linguistic needs (for trade, cultural, scientific and political exchanges) and the aptitude of the population concerned. Thus, the current French government policy favouring "all English" is a fundamental strategic error, demonstrating once again the extent to which the current French elite are living in a world that has already disappeared. But, sadly, it's the peculiarity of parochialism to discover the changes in the world long after they occurred.

These anticipations also bear many implications as regards the EU's political progress since languages are not neutral communication instruments but actually vehicles of visions of the world and society. And through these future trends, one can better make out even bigger changes that will affect the EU project[137].

The progression of the EU's great linguistic balances is, of course, strongly correlated to major global trends in this area[138], but because of its democratic structure and size (500 million citizens), its large linguistic diversity and the antiquity of its languages, the EU is a linguistic expanse which has its own internal coherence, rooted especially in a long history of linguistic interplay.

The EU's linguistic development for the next twenty years is thus determined by two fundamental historical constraints and five strategic factors

Two fundamental historical constraints

1. **The people always ultimately impose their language choices on their elite.**

2. **Languages have international dynamics based primarily on the power and attractiveness of their culture of origin.**

With the disappearance of Latin (from the sixteenth century), to the decline of French (from the nineteenth century) via the ebbing of German (after 1945) and Russian (after 1989), the modern history of Europe continually illustrates the extent to which people have systematically imposed their languages on the elite who, very often, had adopted (more or less freely) foreign languages. The democratic nature of each EU Member State only reinforces this "omnipotence in the duration" of people in linguistic affairs.

The corollary of this constraint is that the opinions and wishes of this same elite in linguistic matters have, de facto, no lasting impact and, for this reason, have no power to plan or anticipate the EU's linguistic future. On the other hand, in an approach particular to the temperament of the "elite", they are generally looking for an identification process that differentiates them from the "people" and are,

---

[137] Of course, beyond the major developments, some specific sectors will now continue to keep such and such a language as a privileged "niche".

[138] In fact, the rise in international strength of Asian languages such as Chinese or Tagalog, or even Arabic, will change global linguistic balances. However, for the next generation, the European international languages will continue to hold significant advantages because they have large linguistic pools outside Europe, particularly in Africa and America. Just as specific sectors will continue to keep such and such a language as a privileged "niche".

therefore, naturally tempted to adopt or use foreign languages that assures them of this differentiation.

The second constraint will usually permit the timing of the development imposed by the first constraint to be defined. The gradual weakening (or sometimes sudden) of the power and attractiveness of the culture underlying a dominant language determines the speed and extent of the new popular choice's rising importance, whether it's the national language, or a new dominant language.

Therefore, these two constraints define the operational framework within which future EU linguistic developments are inscribed.

Five strategic factors

In the EU's case, five key factors will shape the EU's linguistic visage within a generation:

German makes a big comeback

The end of the division of Europe and the reorganization of central Europe resulting in the increasing remoteness of the era of the Second World War are already in the process of promoting a resurgence of German as one of the major trans-European languages between now and 2025. The ongoing democratization of the European Union (increasing importance of public opinion in the EU decision-making process) also directly helps the importance of the German language used by 100 million "natives". All those who manage European networks or projects are already seeing it a little more each day. The use of German in parity with English and French is underway whilst the idea was unthinkable only ten years ago.

The revitalization of the French language

Strong French population growth (and Francophone countries at the origin of a substantial portion of immigration into the EU) already forms a substantial revival of French amongst trans-European languages. With nearly 80 million "native" Francophones, French has, in fact, become the second largest mother-tongue in the EU and continues to grow (for more than a decade France has represented over 60% of the EU's annual natural population growth).

The increasing remoteness of the 1939-1945 period, which marked a collapse of the attractiveness of French as the language of political[139] elite, also works in favour of the French language's return in vitality.

---

[139] Due to the sudden collapse of the "Great Nation" in front of Hitler's forces. However there will be no return to the previous situation because one never fully recovers from a collapse of legitimacy and credibility like that of 1940. The Anglo-Americans are also in the process of discovering this following the Iraqi crisis

The end of Anglo-American as the predominant language of innovation

The end of the world order created after 1945, of which the current collapse of United States' influence is the last act, ends the driving force that brought Europe (and the world) the expansion of the use of English (or more precisely, American). This trend is reinforced by the weakening of Anglo-American in its lands of origin. In the United States, Spanish is rapidly on the rise at the expense of English in many states. In the UK, the increasing importance of the Celtic languages brought on by the demands for autonomy or independence in Ireland, Wales and Scotland have already reversed the use of English in the British Isles (which is already no more than the third mother-tongue in the EU and rapidly diminishing). Over the next twenty years, on the European continent, Anglo-American will remain in force as a plain "international" niche, that is to say, a popular common language, based on a very limited vocabulary.

The Russian language's entry into the "purgatory" of European linguistics

Due to the successive rejection of its brutal administration throughout ex-communist Europe after 1945, Russian will remain, for political reasons, an under-used language in the EU for at least another 10 years. But, assuming a peaceful EU-Russia relationship, eventually reinforced by a successful strategic partnership, the Russian language will establish itself once again as the Slavic common language "par excellence" in the EU from 2015. This change however will probably not be reflected at institutional level (Russian will not become an official EU language) but it will exist de facto and as a reality across the whole of the Eastern part of the EU.

The rise of the Spanish language abroad

The increasing importance of Spanish as a European international language will not be duplicated by its progress as a dominant trans-European language. Indeed, the growing importance of Latin America, and especially the rapid expansion of the Hispanic regions in North America, has led Spanish to becoming one of the three international European languages alongside English and French (also retained by linguistic pools outside the EU). However the low number of Spanish speakers in the EU, the linguistic fragmentation currently taking place in Spain (Basque country and Catalonia) and the presence of another Latin language (French) amongst the dominant trans-European languages, will prevent the Spanish reaching this status.

These trends will be reinforced by the growing communication demands within Europe, characterized by the growing importance of group or individual players

---

and the fact that from being the language of international modernity and truth, Anglo-American has become the language of archaic nationalism and lies.

unable to resort to costly translations and relying heavily on the grasp of what's called a "passive" (understanding) of a foreign language, facilitated by the use of a language in the same linguistic family. Alongside, the other dominant trend will be the increasing use of automatic translation systems in order to circulate multilingual text on a large scale and at low cost.

In conclusion, if the EU's linguistic matrix on the 2020 horizon continues to show itself in the rationale of Umberto Eco's words, "Translation is the language of Europe", a clear linguistic landscape (which will, of course, be tempered by the sectors of activity) emerges, on a background of vivid national and regional languages, highly at odds with the prevailing opinion of the EU elite today[140]:

- Four dominant trans-European languages, English-German-French-Russian, but only three will be official (obviously Russian will not be) and, of which, two will be the EU elite's languages of choice in twenty years (French and German, because Anglo-American will no longer be socially discriminating).

- Three international European languages, English-French-Spanish.

So parents, think carefully well before ticking the boxes for your children's choice of languages!

Value of international university degrees
2010-2020, look out for the crisis in "subprime" degrees!

The global systemic crisis affects all fields and sectors of contemporary human activity. Moreover, it's also what differentiates it from a classic crisis which remains limited to a few sectors and specific regions of the world. The "world after" will, therefore, be characterized by a disruption in the relative value of degrees awarded by the world's major university centres, which became, de facto in a few decades, the equivalent of "international degrees", that's to say having a recognized intellectual, scientific and business value worldwide. The Communist bloc saw such a phenomenon in the 1990s when, suddenly, the value of degrees awarded by prestigious Marxist universities, especially in the USSR, were worth nothing. Today's most valued international degrees face a similar risk in the next ten years. So here are some thoughts to prepare oneself for the global academic landscape of the world after the crisis.

---

[140] Which, as always with the established elite, prove incapable of imagining trends other than yesterday's, namely those on which they founded their status of "elites". That is why the current EU elite continue to believe that the dominant trend of 1980-2000, namely the increase in importance of Anglo-American which has shaped their language skills, will continue.

In a world in full upheaval, prestigious university degrees will also become risky investments!

As one of the fathers of the Erasmus program (which in twenty years changed the European university landscape) [141], I never lost contact with academia in Europe and also the United States, Latin America or Asia. Therefore, it isn't a question of an abstract comparative exercise [142]. There again, it's a question of providing answers to parents and students who are considering investing, sometimes very heavily, in a degree for international purposes hoping to make a successful investment for decades to come in terms of a professional career.

Investing in a degree is, in effect, making a bet on the future at least 10 or 20 years hence. In particular it is assumed that the thousands or tens of thousands of Euros or Dollars invested today will generate a tenfold or hundredfold return in revenue tomorrow. It's a minimum to estimate that the skills developed whilst studying correspond to the requirements and expectations of tomorrow's world. In all cases, for a growing number of parents and students, in the United States, Europe, Asia and the Arab world, it's a big bet on the future.

But the current systemic crisis is in the process of fundamentally changing the absolute and respective values of degrees globally. And strangely, this upheaval is absolutely not reflected in the current dominant discussions on the value of degrees worldwide. However, a decade from now at the latest, some degrees, today at the "top of the academic world", will be greatly devalued. On the contrary, others will see their holders highly sought after by employers.

Think of the graduates of the prestigious Soviet universities before 1989, whose degrees were worthless from the 1990s. An upheaval of the same size is underway which will spread in the years to come. For you or your children do not, today, choose a degree for tomorrow's world from yesterday's!

The world of "prestige degrees" is undergoing the same changes as the planet altogether!

In many respects, the changing world of "prestige degrees" strongly resembles the evolution of the planet itself. After 1945 the emergence of two superpowers, the United States and the USSR, led all the planet's elite to structure their education processes around these two axes. Western universities were developing bilateral tropism almost exclusively with those in America. And in the Communist bloc, Soviet universities became the obligatory rite of passage for satellite regimes'

---

[141] I was indeed fully involved in the U.S. university system in 34 U.S. states between 1999 and 2005, at a time when U.S. universities still had the benefit of healthy budgets. This is no longer the case today when, due to the crisis, they must cut spending on equipment and teaching staff massively.

[142] Many quality studies exist in this area leading to direct recommendations for parents or students.

future executives. This global university "duopoly" imposed its rule over world academia until the 1980s.

From the second half of the 1980s two simultaneous. and not directly correlated phenomena ended this duopoly: the European Community's launch of the Erasmus[143] inter-university programme in 1987 and the Fall of the Berlin Wall in 1989[144]. Although the launch of the Erasmus programme wasn't an historical event of comparable magnitude to the fall of the Berlin Wall, the two phenomena both had the effect of ending the two superpowers' complete domination over international university degrees (that's to say, recognized and accepted beyond their borders).

From the beginning of the 90s, the entire communist bloc's university system, centred on Moscow, was in fact in ruins and the degrees, so popular a few years earlier, weren't worth the paper they're written on in the labour market. At the same time, in a few years, Western Europe, with which the future (and now new) Central and Eastern European member States had rapidly associated themselves, refocused their academic exchanges on Europe and drastically reduced their bilateral exchanges with the United States. To appreciate the magnitude of this development, it is sufficient to note that in the mid 80s, almost 90% of European students who left to pursue a part of their studies abroad went to the United States. Ten years later, in the mid 90s, this proportion had completely reversed and only 10% went to study at an U.S. university whilst 90% of them went to study at a university in another European country.

However, at global university level, given the noisy collapse of the Soviet bloc (as opposed to Erasmus' almost invisible progression), the dominant impression of the 90s was (as in other areas) the acknowledgement of the emergence of a "hyper-power", the United States, whose universities became the undisputed "Meccas" of every brilliant and/or ambitious student whether Arab, Russian, Latin American, Asian or European[145]. American universities also set about maximizing this quasi-monopolistic situation. The most prestigious of them even became exceedingly rich from the revenues generated by overseas students.

But instead of using this position of strength to evolve and adapt to a rapidly changing world, the major U.S. universities were content to profit from this given situation importing at a very high cost renowned academics from abroad. Only a

---

[143] A program that has now aged considerably and which is no longer suited to the European Union's future needs. A short chapter of the book is, incidentally, devoted to this issue.

[144] We say "not directly correlated", because it is clear that Erasmus' launch in 1987 did not cause the fall of the Berlin Wall. However, it seems certain that these two phenomena emerge from a common European dynamic of spontaneously and peacefully rejecting outside control over the "Old Continent". Historical, political and sociological academic studies still remain to be undertaken to analyze this complex phenomenon.

[145] However, this was no longer true of Europeans. Not only were a very small minority involved, but it only involved certain specific sectors such as economics, finance and information technology.

few pioneer institutions tried, with great difficulty, to develop new higher education structures like those which tried to equip NAFTA with a broader aspect of higher education. But these efforts remained marginal because of politicians' disinterest, the "heavyweights" of the herds of U.S. universities[146] and the inability of NAFTA to transcend the status of a simple trade agreement [147].

U.S. university leadership has spent its last major years in the 90s. The flow of foreign students to the United States has collapsed in the last 5 years while they progress on the global level

At the same time "external" tropism dominating major U.S. universities, with less and less American academic staff and students, coincided with a sharp deterioration in the whole of the United States' education system[148]. I place the beginning of this negative development around the period 1970-1975. It has only accelerated under the influence of four converging factors: under-investment in primary and secondary education, race to the bottom via examination procedures based solely on MCQ (Multiple Choice Questions) [149], absence of political authority in charge of the education system and an inability to develop comparative processes with foreign education systems.

It is within this context, structurally very negative, that the events of 11 September, 2001 occurred, then the invasion of Iraq in 2002, causing sustained questioning of the U.S. monopoly over the market for international degrees. First,

---

[146] For an overview of the whole of the university projects and networks that tried to fit themselves into the North American arena, it is useful to consult the database of grants awarded to such projects by FIPSE (Fund for the Improvement of Post Secondary Education), a branch of the U.S. Department of Education, which has been particularly involved in this process.

[147] As highlighted in the 2005-2006 OECD report on Higher Education, the lack of workers' freedom of movement within NAFTA explains to a large extent the dearth of student mobility in North America. Source: "Education Policy Analysis, Focus on Higher Education", OECD, 2005-2006

[148] There is a wealth of specialist American literature on this issue, making the direct link between socio-economic performance and the crisis in education in the United States. I even consider that this degradation can be linked to the widespread use of MCQ and the quantitative assessment of the generations so educated. This is the most direct cause of the intellectual impairment of the whole of the current American elite. The latter have received a distinctly inferior education than the generations that preceded them. It's easy to see when there is an opportunity to frequently discuss or debate with Americans of different generations. The use of only MCQ, combined with excessive quantitative evaluation, have thus created, since the 1970s, two generations fundamentally incapable of doing anything but tick the boxes of a list of tasks. Quite simply, these generations don't know how to ask questions any more, or develop a complex thought because they have not learned to do so.

[149] GW Bush's "No Child Left Behind" programme has further increased the proportion of primary and secondary school pupils of schools (all the young generations as from now) undergoing their entire schooling via a grading based primarily on multiple choice question tests. As well as this system encouraging all the participants in the education system to lower the tests' level of difficulty to improve scores, it bases education on the ability to tick boxes and not to frame questions and work out replies. The impact of this development on U.S. higher education these last two decades is absolutely devastating. Barack Obama has fundamentally challenged nothing here.

measures restricting access to United States' territory, set up in the name of the fight against terrorism, created a legal barrier to entry for many hoping to study in U.S. universities [150]. Secondly, the political, cultural and moral consequences of the invasion of Iraq caused an about turn in the United States' attractiveness among the young elite of the world. The two phenomena reinforce each other, of course, and equally affect the motivation of foreign academics themselves to come and teach in the United States. At the same time, the growing difficulties of the American economy, Katrina and New Orleans, the continued weakening of the U.S. Dollar and the Bush team's budget priorities for defence[151] put a definitive end to the myth of "rich American" universities [152].

At the same time, the formation of a large European world university axe centred around the powerful inter-university networks developed from Erasmus. has led to a proliferation of partnerships between European institutions and universities from other continents (in Unesco's 2004 top 10 global university destinations, there were five European Union countries, the United Kingdom, France, Germany, Spain and Belgium[153]). Asia is also becoming a university destination, necessary because of the continent's increasing global importance.

Since 2006, EU Member States have thereby welcomed twice as many foreign students as the United States (over 1,200,000 against 560,000[154]) and this trend is part of a growing loss of international market share in education by the U.S. universities [155].

All this is reflected of course by very visible developments in statistical terms that show the now steady decline in the number of foreign students going to study in the United States. All continents are affected, even Latin America though geographically the closest [156]. Europe has long ceased sending large contingents to American universities[157] while China and India reshape their flows towards Europe[158] or Australia, when they're not expanding major universities themselves.

---

[150] There are a multitude of articles and studies on this topic.

[151] Particularly to the detriment of research and science.

[152] The increasing number of highly publicized, high-profile killings involving the use of firearms on U.S. university campuses and colleges has not helped to improve the overall image.

[153] Source: « The human face of global mobility: international highly skilled migration in Europe, North America and the Asia Pacific », 2006.

[154] Source: Atlas of Student Mobility, Institute of International Education.

[155] Source: MSNBC, 08/2006.

[156] The Latin American case is well worth analyzing because it is a region of the world that regularly increases the number of its immigrants to the United States and yet, in recent years, the number of Latin American students going to study in the United States is in decline. This illustrates a process of intellectual and cultural "poverty" in the migratory flux to the United States that should concern Washington's highest authorities.

[157] The Latin American case is well worth analyzing because it is a region of the world that regularly increases the number of its immigrants to the United States and yet, in recent years, the number of Latin American students going to study United States is in decline. This illustrates a process of intellectual and

111

Simultaneously, Asia is becoming a major destination of international student mobility with a 213% increase in the number of foreign students in China over the 1999-2005 period, 42% for Australia and 108% for Japan. At the same time, the increase was 17% for the United States, 29% for the United Kingdom, 46% for Germany and 81% for France[159].

This statistical development is of fundamental importance in the medium term for one of the key elements of a professional degree's "value", namely "graduate networks", because it shows that globally the main "graduate networks" of tomorrow will now be formed outside the United States (whereas the reverse was true in recent decades). Moreover, American students themselves now cross the Atlantic in the other direction in large numbers (compared to the 1950-2000 period [160]).

The global systemic crisis involves a profound change in the training requirements of the future international elite

These trends will continue to strengthen as the weakening of the U.S. academic fabric is structural. If it's really linked to the United States' loss of attractiveness in general and to the impoverishment of the country, it equally comes from developments reacting to the emergence of a world different from the one created after 1945, the one for which U.S. universities have formed the global elite over the past six decades. The structure and functioning of the world that is emerging from this global systemic crisis requires elites capable of adapting to the diversity of cultures, civilizations and people. Businesses, government agencies, NGOs and universities themselves are now looking for the skills that can only be acquired by actually comparing the differences, that's to say by a practical experience of other people's world. These organizations are looking for people with the skills to design, manage and develop human and technical networks. Those who have these skills will have a career and will be able to make a return on their degrees.

The "political correctness" that has pervaded the U.S. academic world, the fear of even verbal confrontation that has ensued, the fictional diversity of American campuses against a background of uniform behaviour, increased specialization and a poor level of primary and secondary education, the lack of knowledge and therefore understanding of the rest of the world (though now essential for every

---

cultural "poverty" in the migratory flux to the United States that should concern Washington's highest authorities.

[158] The Americanists are the only one left who believe (or pretend to believe) in some European brain-drain to the U.S., first because they need to justify their submission in the name of some intellectual superiority of the master, and then because, more selfishly, it is a matter of defending the value of their own U.S. diplomas.

[159] Source: "The future of international students in the United States", American Council on Education, 10/2006

[160] Source: " More U.S. students go abroad for their MBAs"», USA Today, 06/06/2007

region of the planet and any occupation, as globalization requires), the obsession with short-term profitability are as much factors that not only don't prepare the student for these indisputable demands on executives for decades to come, but for whom, in fact, the preparation has not been adapted to these requirements by confining him to a view of a virtual world[161].

A command of the working of geographically and culturally diverse networks, practical experience of different cultures, a good knowledge of three or four different languages, interdisciplinary preparation, aptitude to question authority, capable of managing conflict, ability to anticipate collective developments are the definite hallmarks of the elite of these next decades.

At the same time, in scientific training, excellence will remain linked to companies' overall technological[162] performance and cultural excellence[163].

Eurasia (including Russia) at the heart of worldwide academic excellence for the next two decades

Current and lasting trends according to our anticipations (for at least the next twenty years), put Europe and Asia at the heart of the coming scientific, technological and cultural developments. At the same time it is Europe that, for the past twenty years, has confirmed itself as the "centrepiece" of trans-national networks and the champion of multiculturalism. This trend has now resurfaced even in what was long the private hunting ground of U.S. universities, the famous MBA.

So, clusters of tomorrow's academic excellence are in the process of emerging on these two continents, those whose degrees will guarantee the best professional return for two decades to come. However, and this is a radical development compared to recent decades (and a return to the birth of the university in Europe's Middle Ages), excellence cannot come from one institution any more, but from a network of academic institutions. The question a parent or a student must ask themselves in the coming years, is no longer "Has this university a good

---

[161] Moreover, U.S. research is suffering which, despite substantial budget increases, has no longer been able to maintain its share of global innovation in the face of European and Asian competitors since the late 90s. And that even before the crisis began. Source: National Science Foundation, 19/07/2007

[162] And thus for countries or economies having ad hoc technological and industrial bases. Today these are, and will be for at least twenty more years, in Europe and Asia. The de-industrialization of the United States is not, in effect, only a rhetorical figure reserved for American unions.

[163] This clarification is, in our team's view, essential as it comes in contrast to the contention of some existing university centres embodying excellence in a sea of mediocrity. One doesn't grow an elite on infertile soil. In this sense, the great American universities of today have seen their foundations eroded for decades by the degradation of their national educational and cultural environment. Today Berkeley, Harvard, Stamford, etc. are only a pale copy of those 20 or 30 years ago. And in ten years this development will be even more pronounced for the reasons discussed above.

reputation?", but rather "With which establishments of repute does this university collaborate?", "What kinds of common bodies, with institutions in other countries, has this university developed?", etc. It is, in fact, by these links that international academic excellence will now advance in the coming decades.

To avoid being a victim of a crisis in "subprime" degrees ten years from now

However, we continue to read and hear a persistent dominant discussion putting forward U.S. universities as the global "must". This is understandable, even if it's now incorrect, for two simple reasons:

- Those who invested in U.S. degrees over the last thirty years (and they are usually the authors of these analyses) are doing everything they can to maintain their "value".

- Most Asian and European academics of the generation currently holding sway (in their forties and above) continue to consider their career like they did when they were students, that's to say through the prism of the "United States lift". They too are preaching for their parish[164], acting like the "rating agencies/major banks" complex in the current U.S. "subprime" crisis. Changing "hats", they play both the role of "independent" experts, advisors and sellers of the services involved. If you liked the "subprime" crisis, you'll love that of the degrees...

Already, we are seeing two other trends at play that will significantly drive down the quoted value of U.S. university degrees from the first half of the decade: a growing social as well as professional rejection of United States degrees based on the command of finance and management in the short term, a growing (and justified) suspicion that "American style" education is producing an elite who lead projects/businesses straight into "American style" problems that the crisis demonstrates daily [165]. Seriously, to be a graduate of Harvard, Yale or Berkeley in management, finance or law is beginning to be a reason for failure rather than success in finding work outside the United States. For the price that these degrees cost, it's a nasty surprise for those who invested.

---

[164] In Europe, however, it is clear that academics from the Erasmus generation (under 40) have abandoned this view and consider the U.S. "transition" as one stage among others on an international educational circuit. And the two million new European elite formed in twenty years via trans-European degrees will now begin to fully utilize one of the secrets of the value of degrees, namely the "old boy network". Asia is thus in the process of very quickly getting into the same essential stages.

[165] In all these same disciplines, Soviet degrees saw their value collapse after the fall of the Iron Curtain.

Think twenty years hence before investing in a "prestige degree"

In conclusion, parents or students, if you need to invest in expensive higher education in the near future to get a degree with international value, you should know they will cost you much less in Europe for a future professional profitability which is now significantly higher than that of the United States. In Asia, centres of excellence are rising even if their networks are still limited and, therefore, the added-value of their "network" needs to improve further. But this is compensated for by the increasing economic and geopolitical importance of the whole region. The investment in the United States now runs a real risk of a heavy devaluation in a degree's value in line with the loss already actually incurred. And it is unlikely that U.S. academic establishments can initiate significant reforms in the coming years to keep themselves in top shape since the political, economic and financial conditions and human resources (teachers and students) will continue to deteriorate [166].

The pioneers of trans-American university networks are still too few and too weak to influence the whole of this sector in the United States even though it is certainly one of the most innovative academic offerings in the United States. As for the rest, an investment in a U.S. degree is, of course, a useful investment for those who have a calling to make a career in the United States. However, even there, within a decade European and Asian degrees will probably be better respected than any national diploma.

Globalization and the current systemic crisis have thus made the decision to invest in a degree of international value much more complicated. The changes in progress are causing a real upheaval in hierarchies established more than fifty years ago. In this area too, the collapse of the world order created after 1945 primarily affects U.S. institutions and values generated in the United States, a central pillar of the world which is dissolving before our eyes. But as a degree is a twenty year investment at least, one must think the world in 2020-2030 to assess the true value of a degree awarded in the next few years.

2012, European education in the face of the post-Erasmus rendez-vous

But the fall in quality and value of U.S. degrees is not, in itself, a piece of news guaranteeing the quality of European higher education. Indeed, to guarantee their

---

[166] Thus bringing together a mass of U.S. teachers fitted to new educational requirements poses a significant challenge after years of abandonment of the profession and the systematic use of "imported" professors at prestigious universities. The EU for example has chosen to develop the ability to understand the outside world and other cultures by also stimulating the European academic teaching body's trans-European mobility.

presence in the group at the forefront of higher education during 2010-2020, the Europeans must evolve very quickly.

In Europe, there are two very different levels of initiative: primary and secondary which, according to the country, depend solely on the national, regional or local authorities; and higher education whose evolution can only be developed at European level, in a global context. That said, the quality of higher education depends directly on the quality of its secondary education. If a pyramid is built with poor materials, the top will not stay there for long as evidenced by the current U.S. example.

France will therefore find itself faced with two choices that we will finally find in the two scenarios put forward at the end of the book: either it develops, first, a strong voluntary national policy to enhance the quality of primary and secondary education and, secondly, it stimulates an innovative policy of higher education at European level, and it gives itself the means (with other Europeans) to remain at the forefront of learning and knowledge at a global level[167] for the coming decades; or it continues its current policy, copying the U.S. model which has however totally failed, and continues to delude itself in the pursuit of Franco- French academic excellence [168].

The abolition of the teaching of History and Geography in sixth-form science that the French government wants to introduce from 2012 fully illustrates the importance of this connection between the quality of national secondary education and the value of European higher education. In fact, we all know that the vast majority of French higher education science graduates in the coming decades will have to work with foreign colleagues every day. Whether they are engineers in large European or global groups, or researchers in centres operating in European and global networks, almost all of them will have to have the ability to successfully interact well with other cultures, and in particular with European teams. But without a basic knowledge of the history and geography of the countries from where these colleagues come, this essential aspect of successful integration into a multinational team will be missing from French graduates' curriculum.

---

[167] I would add that it has nothing to do with the rantings over 2020 and the economics of intelligence and learning or the knowledge that one sees blooming in Brussels in particular. In fact, I have never heard speak of an economy of stupidity and ignorance as a future project, at least publicly proposed as such. However, I note that the policies implemented in the United States and the United Kingdom for two to three decades, and that the current Parisian elite are now seeking to introduce in France, are aimed at creating less well educated generations, thus contributing to a dumbing down of the population, which thus becomes much more easily manageable.

[168] This is an area where, funnily enough, Americanists and "Gallic alter-fundamentalists" converge since it is to oppose a European dimension. The latter believe in "saving France" when they only plunge further forward into a rationale of standardization on the smallest intellectual common denominator. A sort of NATO in intelligence says it all! Flattering conceit has always been, in fact, an effective tool for losing people.

This will put them at a strong disadvantage compared to graduates from other countries. Today it's sufficient to see how many British figure amongst under-educated graduates in European teams because they have no solid basis in history and geography, to imagine what will happen to French graduates a few years from now if this reform is not cancelled within the next two years. Whether you are engineers or researchers, when you are taken as the cultural laggard of a group (someone who knows neither where cities where people come from are, neither what size they are, nor the principal traits of their cultures), it is not exactly a factor of "excellence". Therefore, our future generations of scientists have a major interest that such a decision should be revoked by the middle of the decade at the latest. Thereafter considerable damage will be caused and one will begin to note it in the divergence between the two scenarios presented at the end of the book.

The great European academic challenge in the years 2010-2020: Putting in place a successor to Erasmus

Moreover, towards the middle of this decade at the latest the EU will have to re-establish its flagship academic program which has allowed it, in the space of twenty-five years, to become a focus of world academia once again. In 2012 it will be, in fact, a quarter of a century since the Erasmus programme was launched involving the renaissance of the European academic circuit and the emergence of the first "massive" core of future European elite. The first "Erasmus generation" will start to have a decisive influence on the levers of power in Europe from the 2010-2020 decade and one of their first tasks will be to rethink European policy on education in a way to face the European Union's dual democratic and management challenge.

In fact, the EU has been in a continuous political crisis for over a decade (and the adoption "against the people's wishes" of the Lisbon Treaty is only a new form of this crisis) since its citizens are not trained to master our society's European dimension and because its elite have stayed national and don't know how to effectively manage the continent. The democratic overhaul of the European Union is through education, by the same path that a million European students have taken since the foundation of the Erasmus student exchange program in 1987.

Today there is a crying need to give the largest possible number of citizens in Europe the chance to become competent European citizens. Everyone needs to understand, propose and act at European level, either alone or with other European citizens. Otherwise our hope of democratizing the EU will remain a dream and the power in the EU will remain in the hands of small groups of elite that can speak several languages, travel easily, build networks across the whole continent and understand European issues prior to them being decided in their place.

The aims of a European policy in the field of education are easy to define:

- Give the young full encouragement to encounter other Europeans and what's necessary to interact with them.

- Allow an increasing number of our students to be trained in a trans - European manner to socially expand and diversify the European elite who can manage the networks, agencies and projects operating at trans-European level. Such training is intended to produce the collective expertise we need to manage the EU democratically, with a "European savoir-faire" spread throughout society and not reserved for a handful of bureaucratic structures and consulting firms.

- Integrate the European dimension into higher education's regular curriculum.

It is important to emphasize that this is not a "European education policy" through which the European level would order or influence the content and process of education in Europe. Such an attempt would be doomed to failure because it would negate the national characteristics that make the very richness of the cultural fabric of Europe. Education policy will remain national, regional or local. It would, in fact, be a threat to democracy and cultural diversity, a single power controlling the operation, or even having an important influence on the content and methods of education of 500 million people from very different cultures.

On the other hand, the definition and implementation of a "European policy on education" consisting of a series of flexible and future-oriented programs and projects, is essential for the democratic future of the EU. A quarter of a century after the founding of the Erasmus programme, it will transform this path into a series of lanes adapted to the public and time with goals as diverse as the EU has become complex. Expand this program, diversify it, and adapt it to the European Union's new political, economic, social and cultural challenges of the next two decades, here's what's needed.

Having been behind Erasmus' adoption, I know that national or regional bureaucracies may be tempted to fight against trans-European programs in the education field. Just as Member States' education ministries fought against the Erasmus programme in 1985-1987, because they did not want to open up Europe in their field, to prevent comparisons, the development and reform of their old structures. The same may be true for some players today. In France, here again, one will find the unnatural collusion of the Americanists and superannuated Gallic alter-fundamentalists, who will attempt either to direct French higher education towards the United States, or to dangle a purely Franco-French reform in front of it.

One is, in fact, right in the middle of this process. The Eurotechnos are now silent and lost for ideas because they haven't any political visionaries or bold technocrats[169] anymore and because imagination is not really their strongpoint. The other two groups can therefore devote themselves to it to their heart's content. But reality places strict limits on historical mistakes. The younger generation does not share the Americanists' transatlantic dream, and they are a bit cramped in the national jar. For this reason we can bank on a revival of the European higher education policy between now and the middle of the decade. Moreover, the recent EU decision to launch a European assessment system of the world's major higher education institutions is a crucial first step in this direction. The University of Shanghai's ranking, which until now is the leading authority on the subject, is in fact, a puppet of the U.S. universities and whose sole purpose is to promote their own product[170].

European policy in this area must be organized around three simple ideas:

- **A goal of mobility for each generation**
  Each Member State must acquaint at least 10% of each new generation each year with other Europeans. Every two years, the European government must give a report to the European Parliament to assess the results of each Member State in relation to this 10% target. This discourse will be public and Parliament will establish a list of the most active countries benefiting their citizens from this European dimension.

- **Two new major European programmes**
  The first must be of a sufficiently large size, serving the EU's democratization by a better education of its citizens in Europe, the other more elitist, again serving the EU's democratization, by better educating its senior staff in the dimension of Europe. The concept of a three to six months' course in another European university (copying Erasmus) must itself become an integral part of higher education's regular curriculum and therefore be funded at national and/or regional levels[171].
  The first will target the young aged from 10 to 25 years (secondary to higher level), aiming to train tomorrow's Eurocitizens, acquainting them with other Europeans, making them comfortable with Europe and its diversity by offering them the bases of intra-European democratic dialogue (knowledge of others,

---

[169] In France especially this pool, so rich, that has fueled the human resources of the EU's construction period in 1950-1970 has now dried up because all these brilliant elite have gone to work in the private sector.

[170] It is some sort of rating agency for universities. The creation by the EU of a concurrent rating agency in this field gives an idea of chat this decade could bring in financial terms too.

[171] European programmes are intended to break new ground in European integration. Once the way has been signposted, like Erasmus, it's for those at national and regional levels to take over, spread the policy widely and free up the means for a new European advance.

119

language, etc.). Without necessarily going through the education system, the method will be based on short visits, exchanges, meetings (three days minimum to one week maximum) with an annual target of 500,000 young people per year. With one hundred million Euros per year in financial support, it's an inexpensive investment[172] in the future and very profitable, especially if it is measured against the hundreds of billions made available to the banks in 2008-2009, which was only intended to pay for the past.

The second program will aim to train each year the tens of thousands of European executives that our country and the EU need. Its target will be, of course, students and academia to compensate for the growing shortage and train European executives capable of managing businesses, public services, universities, media, NGOs and research centres across the EU and thus be able to confront the conditions of the multi-polar world after the crisis. The central scheme will be based on the principle of integrated curricula, already widely tested for a decade, including at least three terms spent in three different member states and a term spent in another major region of the world[173]. This would involve about fifty thousand students per year, at an annual cost of about forty million Euros. It will, of course, be more expensive per "head" than the previous program.

• Integrate the European dimension in the higher education curriculum

This objective is in fact the sustainability and general implementation of Erasmus by making it compulsory, to obtain a university degree, to have spent some months studying in another European country or have a bi-national degree validated by two universities in two different countries. The costs of these measures must be borne by the bodies who fund higher education in each member state because, in the coming decades, no higher education graduate will be able to aspire to a position of responsibility without having a minimum European experience. This is not an opinion but a simple statement about the reality of the European job market.

Moreover, it will be necessary to define a common framework for learning languages during this decade which will see the idea of a common European language through the medium of Anglo-American fade away. It can rely on a policy of encouraging bilingual education in popularizing the teaching of a foreign language from the age of four years, by empowering Member States and regions with financial support. The main threads of such a measure are simple however and already tested on a large scale in many European institutions: target children from four years old by allowing pupils to open their minds to Europe by acquiring a

---

[172] In the order of magnitude of an average-sized EU programme.

[173] This will be, especially, a means of preserving the EU's central position in the field of international academic networks.

second language and exposure to another culture, encourage the provision of financial support to teach two languages to the youngest and bilingual schooling for the eldest, because young children mustn't "study" a language, but find a natural way of learning it and understand the culture that goes with it. They must be exposed and led to use it hence the importance of using foreign language assistants from the countries of the language being taught, of establishing an "exchange" of language assistants (internet) to help match supply and demand, and encourage the mutual recognition of qualifications for schools and infant school teachers as well as the training of "bilingual teachers".

The decade when Islam converts to Europe

The past decade, with attacks of the 11th September, in London and Madrid, the collapse of the American multicultural model (adopted in the 1970s by the North Europeans), the Danish crisis of Muhammad's cartoons, the increasing use of anti-Muslim rhetoric by the far-right parties and discussions on immigration which are its "civilized" version for most European parties of the right[174], the escalation of Islamic extremists in Europe and the Muslim world has been marked by a very violent interaction between the West and Islam, both taken over by extremists.

In Europe, the Americanist lobbies such as that in power in France at the beginning of the decade, fully utilize these trends to push forward their vision of a West in direct conflict with the Islamic world. That also serves as a conduit for their security alternatives thanks to the terrorist threat and allows attention to be diverted from the economic crisis by discussing issues of identity, an inward-looking and therefore irresistible subject "par excellence".

Yet in reality, as opposed to the media's distorting summarization, one sees a clear trend taking shape that will brand the decade provided that Europeans know how to manage it well. The vast majority of Muslims on our continent are beginning to clearly understand that in Europe Islam must learn to be a religion like any other, essentially limited to private life and subject to compliance with the law and democratic principles, including freedom of expression.

Of course there are, in effect, forces in the Muslim world that haven't yet accepted this basic fact that determines the progress of this religion on our continent. Let's take three examples: the Danish cartoons of Mohammed, the French law against headscarves in schools and the Swiss referendum against minarets.

---

[174] As clearly demonstrated by the discussion on French identity launched by Nicolas Sarkozy's team.

The ban on headscarves in French schools and the absence of minarets on mosques in Switzerland are the first elements of framing Islam in a European religious context, which by its secularism is earnestly concerned to avoid any proactive intrusion into the public arena by one religion or another. A minaret or a scarf both belong to this clear and asserted intrusion into the public arena. In prohibiting them the French and Swiss do nothing other than affirm the importance of the neutrality of this public space. In both cases, thurifers of multiculturalism, which has never had a future in Europe except to produce Geerd Wilders, de Villiers and others, announced serious unrest and radicalization of Muslims in the countries involved. However, absolutely nothing happened. Evidence that the decisions, whilst not being appreciated, have been understood by the vast majority of French and Swiss Muslims.

Regarding the cartoons of Mohammed, we touch on an extraneous dimension of the European relationship to religion in a world where information travels very quickly now. Every European has the right to caricature Mohammed like Jesus., Moses or Buddha, or again the Pope, the Queen of England, the President of the French Republic, or homosexuals, the disabled, animal lovers, environmentalists, communists, blondes, Belgians, the French, Germans, Americans, Russians, Africans, Arabs, Jews, those from the Auvergne, Scots or even his own neighbour. If there is a prejudice, it's for the courts to decide, and not such and such a religious authority or a small activist group. The vast majority of five hundred million European citizens are attached to this right that has taken centuries to wrest from their kings and priests. There is, of course, no question of limiting it. It's even one of Europe's strengths that is capable of generating a sufficient uproar to upset other civilizations, ideas, concepts and political models as I mentioned earlier.

Europeans have not taken centuries, often deadly, to reach a settled balance, satisfactory for the vast majority of their fellow citizens, to suddenly agree to it being challenged by religious fundamentalists who want to see their law, prohibiting the depiction of Muhammad, binding on all those who do not believe in their religion. In Europe, it is not religion that makes the law, it is the people, through majority votes, and according to democratic principles accepted by the vast majority of the continent's people. If it is clear that there is no legitimacy to provoke this or that group on its core beliefs (religious, philosophical, sexual, or other) when there is no infringement of the law, in Europe the cartoon is free to choose the target it wants.

Moreover, the zealots of the non-representation of the prophet of Islam are often the same people who invoke his name rightly or wrongly, attaching his "legitimacy" on the slightest attack they perpetrate, on the least claim that they make. On these occasions, they seem far less cautious about the orthodoxy, and the believers then seem far less willing to rebel against any hijacking of the spirit and text of their religion. So, let's not be manipulated by the so-called "impact" of these cartoons on the majority of Muslims, especially when it comes to those who live in Europe. Their vast majority is silent because they really must wonder what it's all about. So, let's leave aside the professionals of the alleged irreducibility of Islam to modernity or secular European environment[175], and look at the reality of the next decade and see how Islam is in the process of integrating itself into the European religious fabric.

In mid-December 2005, I had the opportunity to participate in a lengthy discussion with 25 specialists and experts of Islam at the Hebrew University of Jerusalem, on the theme "Europe, France and Islam". During these very full exchanges, I had to remind the power relations that exist between Europe and Islam, particularly as to the supposed impossibility of adaptation of this religion.

With 500 million people concentrated on a "small piece of land", the EU can have a big impact on the progression of a religion that only has three times as many believers scattered across several continents. Especially as within the EU, Islam is certainly a growing religion, but in a very small minority (about 20 million believers). In effect, Europeans will put a lot of pressure on Muslims so that they understand that in Europe, Islam must act like other religions, and remain strictly limited to the private realm, while accepting the law and democratic principles. So it is a major common challenge that awaits all Europeans and their Muslim compatriots. How to adapt through education, integration and discussion (and necessarily, sometimes, by argument too) Islam to a secular European context? It is a difficult path, which will see fundamentalists of all sides trying to obstruct. Because from the Christian or Jewish side, there are also trends that really want to see religions again becoming the wellhead of law as they were in Europe until the Renaissance and which see the incidents with Islam as the chance to push forward their own ambitions.

This is also why we must be vigilant. As I reminded my interlocutors in Jerusalem, no one should forget that Europe, and Europeans, have a "dark side" that is suddenly capable of generating the worst: expulsions, pogroms, massacres, death camps. The list is long. However, I believe that the continuous rise in influence of extremist and xenophobic forces on our continent for twenty years or so marks the return of this "dark Europe", muzzled after 1945. Moreover, it has been one of my ongoing aims these last twenty-five years to successfully oppose these forces of exclusion, by embodying a new political option, democratic, open, built to our continent' scale, on the level at which these forces operate too. However, one mustn't tempt the "devil" (talking about religion!) and let it feed the forces of extremism by leaving the way open to the attitudes and discussions that find it abnormal that a newspaper should publish a cartoon of Mohammed or which consider that, on the contrary, they are justified in enhancing the religious architectural presence of our cities. Muslim fundamentalists and followers of

---

[175] And many in the "politically correct" camp maintain this type of historical pap. Those are really unforgivable because they are not even believers.

"politically correct multiculturalism" are the best friends of those who dream of a return to an intolerant Europe.

Moreover, European Muslims would be the first victims. Because in such a case, European destiny would again model itself on old patterns, and lead Europeans to a new bloody madness of mass expulsions or anti-Muslim carnage. Clearly, in Jerusalem, these phrases ring out more loudly than in Europe, because Muslims or Jews, from the Crusades to the Holocaust, are aware of this latent European barbarism.

But they must also strongly resonate in Europe so that we can maintain this delicate balance that allows Europeans of all religions, and no religion, to coexist peacefully within a common society. To succeed, by integration, education, discussion, it is essential not to succumb to the ease of cultural relativism, to the fiction that there would be legitimate self-proclaimed characteristics, to the intellectual terrorism of the "politically correct".

Islam in Europe will, therefore, be a European Islam, that is to say, framed by the limitations and constraints that Europeans apply to all religions or else, it will not be. As I reminded those in Jerusalem, we shouldn't delude ourselves in order to avoid tragic mistakes. If, in the middle of this decade, we want to avoid the history of Europe finding the paths that led Europeans to the worst in the last century, it is imperative we make this difficult, but honest and fair, choice, respecting our principles and aware of our limitations.

Progressive forces in Europe no longer have a future at national level

The 2010-2020 decade will be a period of major transition in world history, as the global systemic crisis requires. It will also be fundamental in terms of European Union politics because the combination of the global crisis, the end of the unipolar world based around the United States and the arrival in power of the first European generations born after the ratification of the Treaty of Rome will lead all progressive forces in Europe to ask this simple question: Have the forces of progress in Europe still a future at national level?

In effect, if the current crisis has its roots in the imbalances and excesses of the last twenty to thirty years, the emergence of trans-European political forces dates back about 25 years (and the revival of the Community project in 1984-85). This coincidence of time reflects, in my opinion, a strong historical trend marked by the rise in influence of a dual process of internationalization:

- On the one hand the globalization of trade

- On the other the regionalization of politics.

In both cases the nation-state is the victim of the process, stripped of its essential powers and sentenced to only give an illusion (especially by its leaders' hyper-agitation).

The current crisis illustrates how, despite the announcements of so-called "stimulus plans", European states are now minor players. And so let's not be mistaken on "EU impotence", it's the Commission, the European Council and European Parliament who are impotent, due to a lack of political legitimacy and concrete authority. On the other hand the European Central Bank calls the tune and tomorrow, in reply to the worsening global crisis, the Eurozone's Member States will have to create a real political secretariat backed by a government debt agency common to the entire Eurozone exempifying the marginalization of national power. Besides, if there is really one thing that has become clear to all in terms of European collective interest it is, thanks to this historic crisis, that "outside the Eurozone, there is no salvation" (as the race to the Euro by all the Euro-skeptic countries of the past decade illustrates).

The likely fragmentation of the global market from now into a series of regional blocs will accentuate national economic and financial break up in the EU, consecrating a fact which has become obvious to any vigilant observer of political life in Europe for the last twenty years: The power has become European. Economic, financial, strategic, diplomatic and regulatory power and henceforth therefore, in times of crisis, social and political power as well.

This leads us to the second part of this argument. Politics being nothing more than the conquest and use of power, those who do it to try and change things in the public interest (the best definition in my view of the concept of "progressive forces") need to urgently settle the question of power in Europe. Where is the power now? Always at the national level? Or has it now passed to a European level (knowing that its global aspect fades away as the crisis continues to develop)?

The above explanations allow a clear answer to this question. In Europe now, power is no longer at national level, it has moved to the European level. This should therefore lead the continent's progressive forces to draw an honest conclusion vis-à-vis their constituents and members. The public must stop being deceived into believing that the national political parties and national elections are the central power stakes. We must instead construct trans-European political forces that enable, around the election of the European Parliament and a series of trans-European political actions, to create the tools, skills and democratic legitimacy to control power at European level instead of leaving it, like today, only in the hands of lobbyists and bureaucrats.

For the power to change reality in order to improve the situation of the greatest number and serve the collective interest, requires the control of power where it is and not where one prefers to think it is. Of course, this means making painful sacrifices, such as building new political forces, like telling the truth to its supporters and voters (who, in fact, are starting to notice it on their own) over the impotence of progressive national parties. But nobody ever said that the conquest and exercise of real power was a walkover.

Of course conservative forces, those which, to the left or right of the political spectrum in each of our countries, don't want to change much in fact, are perfectly happy with this fiction of national competition for a power which has now moved on up to European level, out of national reach. Anyway, they generally prefer power should be in the hands of groups outside the democratic arena.

But for the others, who want citizens to have a real influence on our collective future, those who want to be able to progress our societies for the benefit of the greatest number, isn't continuing to "vote national" a real betrayal of their hopes, desires and beliefs? In 2010, in the midst of an historic crisis, with a single currency and market in particular, the question is worth asking.

In conclusion, women and men who genuinely wish to change society in the interests of the greatest number should ask themselves very specific questions: Is it honestly the best way to change society by voting or campaigning for a national party, with its national program and with its vision limited to national issues? Will this national party be able to understand, anticipate and resolve the major problems facing us in the years to come? Or will it be condemned, and us with it, to be powerless and turn out to be impotent jettisoning the mistakes on Europe and the rest of the world? Quite simply, can one still be honestly progressive in politics in Europe in the 2010-2020 decade, and only vote or campaign for a national party?

To me, that seems difficult at least. Since the political temperament abhors a vacuum, this power which has now moved up to European level will inevitably generate political forces to use it. It's probably in the middle of the decade now beginning that this development will accelerate ending up with real trans-European political struggles at the end of the decade. Both accounts of the future reveal two very different winners depending on whether the world and Europe follow a tragic path or just a very painful one.

EU 2020, towards polycentrism and the end of the 1950s triangle

For twenty years, the geographic base of European institutions has been in the process of freeing itself from the Brussels-Luxembourg-Strasbourg triangle that the founders of the Community project of the 1950s temporarily left. Whatever European leaders think, this trend will accelerate in the 2010-2020 decade and lead

126

the EU to experiment with a new institutional geography, blending roots in history and innovation in governance. Beyond the organizational aspect, it's a development that is also part of the requirement for greater EU democratic legitimacy and therefore the greatest proximity to its citizens.

Rationalize a geographic development already underway

The choice of Frankfurt as the European Central Bank's host city is the clearest demonstration of this trend. In fact, taking into account the choices made at the beginning of the Construction, an institution as important as the ECB should have been automatically located in one of the institutional triangle's three cities. However, this option was not even mentioned. It goes without saying that the "best city" had to be found for a Central Bank of the EU. And it is interesting to analyze the requirements for the choice of Germany and Frankfurt, which was obvious in a way as much for Europeans judging the finance role compatible with Germany's image, as for Germans welcoming this institutional EU structure with interest and pride.

The transfer of certain European Commission functions and their relocation to "peripheral" cities is another sign, already even older (late 80s), of this trend of EU institutions to move closer to European citizens, with the dual aim of better matching national institutional and vocational functions and to improve the institution's image of an "Ivory Tower". The European Environment Agency, for example, has been transferred to Copenhagen. It should be noted that even at the time of the founding fathers, the choice of the EEC capital didn't cover a single city. From the outset, the European Community's very nature required, therefore, the concept of a network of capitals. However the needs and options in this area have changed so much in 50 years that it would almost be a betrayal of the spirit of the Founding Fathers not to take it into account within the framework of thought on EU institutional reform.

Paradoxically, technological developments (especially the TGV and Internet) reinforce the natural centres of activity and power. They work in favour of an actual decentralization, but in the middle of a space without borders, where it's the most dynamic and powerful centres of activity which assert themselves as the essential nodes in the flow of knowledge, power, influence, finance and culture. This development increases the distance between these "nodal" megacities and the others, showing how much European institutions, de facto, put themselves on the fringe by being located outside this network.

As regards the private sector, we are seeing that an increasing number of multinationals have chosen to have several headquarters, dedicated to different tasks (R&D, customers, production, etc.), in different cities and countries, choosing to operate as a network. For instance Shell, after consideration, decided to retain its dual-headquarters (London and The Hague) because of its Anglo-Dutch history, rather than having just one. Knowing that the private sector, limited by objective factors of profitability and efficiency, is a good gauge of changes in the approach to organization and work, it's fair to ask oneself to what extent the reasons for this development are equally valid for European public institutions.

Give the EU credible capitals to take on the challenges of the twenty-first century

These new kinds of developments unquestionably represent a change in the nature, one acknowledged by all, of the European entity as such and its natural environment. There is no doubt that between the fall of the Berlin Wall, the Maastricht Treaty, the changeover to the Euro and the expansion to over 25 members, the European Union is nothing like the Economic Community of the 50s. The economic powerhouse that Europe has become, thanks to the success of the founding fathers' project, has profoundly changed the entity's nature, the challenges it must now pit itself against and therefore the tools it needs to acquire, especially for fully using its potential political status in this crucial decade.

The themes of EU democratization, institutional legitimacy, connecting with citizens, are now at the heart of any thinking on Europe's future. So far this debate has remained largely theoretical in the absence of a functioning anchor point. How to legitimize an institution without questioning it fundamentally? How to get closer to citizens without moving the institutions? We can see how get the institutions closer to the citizens, whilst it's difficult to see how to bring 500 million citizens closer to the institutions. In fact choosing, as the EU's institutional heart, a network of capitals like London, The Hague, Bonn, Cologne, Paris, Frankfurt, Brussels, Rotterdam, Amsterdam, Luxembourg, etc. would de facto bring Europe closer to nearly 200 million Europeans (an essential legitimate base).

The reinforcement of the EU's place in the world is another challenge which now confronts Europe. How to declare the existence of Europe in relation to the outside world when the benchmark cities are Brussels, Luxembourg or Strasbourg which nobody has ever heard of? How to give the image of a strong entity when the outside world can hardly locate its capitals geographically, culturally or historically? A strong entity is rooted in strong cities. After the fall of the Berlin Wall, one of Germany's first steps, to show everyone its rediscovered unity and greatness, was to move its institutions from Bonn to Berlin.

The EU is the world's leading trade and second economic power. But to remain so, competition is fierce. In particular, to deal with the groupings of "Kyoto-Tokyo", "Los Angeles-San Francisco" or "Boston-New York-Philadelphia", the EU needs to strengthen and develop a "global conurbation" capable of being a vital link in the economy, research, finance and culture globally. Only one region can play this role, the EuroRing "London-Glasgow - Delta Metropolis[176] - Rhein Gebiet[177] - Paris-Ile de France" that can be designated as the "North West European Conurbation". In effect, as well as States combining to create competitive economic centres, major cities are a second level of unification still poorly exploited at trans-national level.

The problem of recruitment and human resources has been a serious and recurring problem for EU organizations for a decade now. Due to their location, these cities haven't got pools of employment to the extent needed by these establishments (whether it be recruitment for the long term or shorter missions). Being far from the major centres of state-of-the-art skills in the fields of science, finance, economics, politics and culture, they fail to attract the high-level personnel they need, despite the attractiveness of the salaries. This situation is going to get worse due to the worsening image and status of these institutions over a number of years. Moreover, this situation increasingly generates "incestuous" hiring practices where members of the same family hold positions in the same organization or in those located in the same city.

The magnitude of this phenomenon naturally strengthens the opacity and remoteness of these organizations while reducing their collective expertise. Thus in human resource terms, relocating in the EuroRing zone with a large pool of employment, could bring a double benefit, allow recruitment of those with the best skill levels and equalize and expand recruitment at the centre of these institutions by preventing the process of "family grouping" within these same EU organizations.

The cities' place and role in the EU structure have, more than ever, been given a new popularity. In effect, it has gradually become clear that the cities are the "missing link" in EU integration. European institutions, states and citizens are systematically mentioned as the players and future players (in the case of citizens) of European construction in the twenty-first century. But the discussion on institutional reform does not include cities, or only hardly or badly. This is because the right connection has not yet been found: twin-towns in Europe (top-down), but artificial, or lobby-cities in Europe (bottom-up), but for very local interests. Euro-Ring, consisting of establishing the EU in its major historic cities, seems like an answer to the question of connecting cities and the EU project.

The growing weakness of the States' stature in the EU contest also contributes to weaken the capital cities chosen in the 50s because they were a choice of the States.

---

[176] Amsterdam, The Hague, Rotterdam, Utrecht

[177] *Cologne, Bonn, Frankfurt*

Take advantage of the opportunities offered by new technologies
« Because being isolated is also not to use the means that exist to be closer »

Relatively recent developments have indeed radically altered the environment and methods of working:

- High-speed transport has considerably changed the travel map of Europe with shorter journey times and increased mobility. At the moment London, Brussels, Paris, Cologne, Bonn, Frankfurt and The Hague are within 3 hours of each other. Competition in Europe from the TGV is gradually leading airlines to also offer extremely cheap fares, thus contributing to the democratization and furtherance of intra-European connections. The limitations that prevailed in the 50s on the choice of grouping of organisations around a very tight triangle no longer apply in the same way. It is now easy to envisage an even greater decentralization of European institutions without compromising their staff or delegates' quality of work.

- New technologies are, of course, the other revolution of the last decade in terms of working patterns. The Internet and e-mail have eliminated any notion of distance by the ability to find information, connecting to any organization, communicating with colleagues, remote working, on a network. With these new tools, there is no longer any reason to be in the same city to work better, it has become easier to communicate with one's office colleagues by e-mail than by talking to them. The Internet has even helped to define this trend called "meeting-itis" which appeared in the early 90s in response to changing methods of networking, and ended by causing a loss of valuable time. If real meetings are still essential, they have changed in their usefulness. Monday's board meeting is better replaced by sending an in-house newsletter by email to all employees (new applications appear daily in this area).

- Finally, organization fashions have changed in nature in recent decades, moving from the pyramid to network model. This change, related to a triple constraint of efficiency, complexity and democratization of all professional activity, has encouraged significant changes in the very structuring of businesses and government services. The pyramids flatten, expand; the levels of the pyramid give way to the roles of a network, complementarities appear, organizations clearly divide themselves into complementary but autonomous entities. This rational "explosion" of organizations is easily translated physically into an organization's decentralization and geographic deployment.

Thus we begin to see the early stages of development of an European institutional network, in two concentric rings, capable of blending future EU institutional-geographical developments together (enlargement, political and institutional development ...): Euro-Rings.

130

Admitting that the choice of capitals is critical to the nature of a political entity

Three examples should clarify this issue:

Berlin
We have already mentioned the exceptionally significant instance of Germany's change of capital at the time of the fall of the Berlin Wall. This example shows the extent to which the choice of capital and the historical characteristics of the nature of the entity they represent are linked. And a question at the heart of the Euro-Rings project is to properly distribute the institutional functions between the cities with good judgement.

The Netherlands
The Netherlands provide another interesting context of the different forms that can encase places of power. In effect, as everyone knows, the Netherlands hasn't one, but three or even four capitals: The Hague, Amsterdam, Rotterdam and Utrecht, which continuously configure their respective advantages. The Hague is the institutional capital, Rotterdam is the economic capital and Amsterdam is the cultural capital. Utrecht has just been recently incorporated into this Dutch conurbation with the object of completing an economic centre, the Delta Metropolis, which is likely to compete with the major European and world capitals. The Dutch system is full of lessons on a model of networked capitals, the link between economics and politics, on the importance of the visibility of places of power and on each city's specialization.

Luxembourg
The choice of Luxembourg in 1952 as the headquarters of the High Authority of the ECSC can be described as the perfect example of « Community » compromise, unconnected with any symbolic democratic or historical consideration. This choice was necessary « because everybody was tired » and Luxembourg worried nobody. However, it's on this kind of « horse-trading » that the EU institutions' geographical structure is still based today.

These few examples show that the choice of an entity's capital and the forms it can take correspond largely to its nature: an institutional entity (ECSC), a politico-economic entity (Delta Metropolis), a political entity (Berlin) choose the capitals that represent them best. A choice that deserves much attention because it subsequently shapes the entity it represents. Undeniably, the EU has reached a stage of development that requires another choice of its capital(s) on grounds incorporating democratic, historical, political, demographic and economic factors and the necessity of efficiency. This will be one of the major works of the upcoming decade and probably the following.

131

The first EuroRing is materializing before our eyes with high-speed trains that have spontaneously connected London-Paris-The Hague and Frankfurt in a circle around Brussels. We are already seeing the dawn of the second EuroRing of Copenhagen, Stockholm, Barcelona, Milan, Prague, Budapest and Warsaw which make up the "second wave" of cities connected at high speed. A European power that is both effective and close to the ground can be embodied along these lines and around these rings. As always for major strategic issues it's the management that makes the difference in the long run, not the aspirations of such and such a bureaucrat or political leader.

As announced at the beginning of this book, after the challenges of the world and Europe, I chose to present two scenarios of global change in the 2010-2020 decade. They represent the two extremes between which that change will probably take place. You will notice that neither of the two, even the more positive, is "brilliant". I do not believe that tomorrow will be a better day but, on the other hand, I know that with an early collective awareness and the assertion of strong will, we will be able to avoid the worst and, with difficulty, build a better world at the end of the current historical crisis. But, sadly, there is only one opportunity.

Two narratives of the future 2010-2020

I wanted, therefore, to give a "face" to the 2010-2020 decade. There are in fact "two faces" as the first scenario presents a series of events representative of the trends that can allow the emergence of the "world after" from the middle of the decade onward, while the second shows what a decade in which "the world before" tries to delay the historic changes underway by any means it could. I want to emphasize again that the events and dates are indicative. I do not claim to be able to predict the future. Of course, the reality will match neither one nor the other scenario, but on the other hand I think that the history of the next ten years will be written somewhere between these two alternatives.

These narratives are a way of making conceptual analyses more explicit and to illustrate their possible sequences. For example, it is clear that I do not know when Belgium's present king will die. But, on the other hand, I am convinced that his death will sharply accelerate the country's division. Similarly, if certain events seem "huge" for dates so close, I'll just mention two compelling stories:

In 1988 and 1989, people considered my analysis of the collapse of the Soviet Union within a decade and the need, therefore, for the European Community to prepare for an inevitable reunification of Germany, to be completely fanciful. In fact, it only took a few months for it to happen. In February 2006, I was widely criticized by "experts" when I signed LEAP's announcement of the imminent outbreak of the global crisis which we are seeing now. These last few years have proved to us that when history accelerates, its speed is amazing. Now, I will say once again, a crisis like the one we are living through is, more than anything else, a tremendous acceleration of history.

So, fasten your seatbelts and start discovering two portrayals of the 2010-2020 decade [178].

---

[178] Both narratives are mainly concerned with aspects of geopolitical and macroeconomic developments. They reflect the trends developed in the analyses and anticipations in this book. They assume an absence of any major technological, political or moral innovation able to radically change the way our societies function between now and the end of the decade. Thanks to LEAP's help, the second narrative, the most tragic, was tested on several thousand of its readers. The reactions, coming from all continents, have been very positive and helped to refine its content.

1. The painful dawn of the "world after"

2010: Direct conflict between the U.S.A / EU / Asia to attract global savings insufficient to finance the growing deficits / Inability coupled with a growing lack of enthusiasm by China, Japan and the Gulf oil kingdoms to buy the mountain of U.S. Treasury bonds created by the exponential U.S. deficit / Unveiling of the massive hidden repurchase of U.S. Treasury Bonds by the Fed / Increasing purchases of gold by central banks around the world / Acceleration in the rise of unemployment throughout the world (levels of 20% in the United States and Europe) / China's growth falls below 5% again / Refusal of American and European governments to increase the tax burden on the richest 10% / The United Kingdom government is forced to cut of public sector pensions by 50% and civil servants' salaries by 20%.

2011: Increasingly difficult G20 meetings (like the Copenhagen Summit) resulting in meaningless press releases / Washington refuses to organize a G20 meeting in Moscow - G20 meeting takes place in Tokyo / United States unemployment rate over 20 % / Enlargement of the grassroots anti-Fed and anti-Wall Street movement / Daily riots of migrant workers in China / Implementation of a European Solidarity Fund to help regions most affected by unemployment and putting public finances in Spain, Ireland, Italy and Greece in order / Daily demonstrations and strikes in major European cities / Spain's unemployment rate reaches 30% of the workforce / Faced with market distrust, the United Kingdom is obliged to borrow from the IMF to balance its 2010 budget / Angela Merkel agrees to a supplementary three year tax on 10% of the richest taxpayers / In France the UMP calls for the removal of the tax shield against the advice of President Sarkozy leading to a government crisis and a coalition of the right led by François Fillon / Collapse in tax revenue in the United States, many states like Texas and California refuse to remit tax receipts to the Federal Government / Growing doubts about the exact amount of United States gold reserves / Increasing number of anti-federal attacks in the United States perpetrated by extreme right-wing militias / Recognized NATO failure in Afghanistan - Withdrawal of European troops / Increasing number of referenda and regional decisions in Europe against Islam's external features: veil, burka, minaret.

2012: The United States announces the withdrawal of all their troops from Iraq and Afghanistan / Growing disruption of the global economic fabric (production lines for many products interrupted by the collapse of vital links) / Return of trading and economic blocs based on the refusal to implement WTO rulings /

135

Relocation of environmental issues in the economic and geopolitical domain of influence / European threats to impose heavy customs duties on products deemed too polluting in their manufacturing process / Increasingly erratic movements of the U.S. dollar / The United States obliged to pay a 10% interest rate to sell their Treasury Bonds / The BRIC countries, Saudi Arabia and the Eurozone, announce the holding of a G20 emergency summit in Beijing / Washington and London refuse to participate / The British pound collapses 50% against major international currencies / London finally participates in the G20 extraordinary summit / Putin elected Russia's new President / Obama is defeated by a Republican pragmatist / Strauss-Kahn is elected French President / The question of a new global benchmark currency is put at the top of the agenda at the Beijing G20 meeting / The IMF is given the responsibility for coordinating the preparatory work for a new international benchmark currency, including the timescale for its launch and the method of its management / IMF internal voting power is fundamentally changed contingent on major regional balances: Europe 20%, North America 17%, Asia 40%, Latin America 13%, rest of the world 10%.

2013: Establishment of a Global Monetary Institute, originating from the IMF and the group of central banks whose currencies make up the basket of currencies and the launch of a global competition over the Internet to choose its name[179] / Setting exchange rates between each currency and the new global benchmark currency / Putting in place of a global financial regulatory framework / Success of the Nice Brice Summit (BRIC + Europe) [180] / Move towards a stabilization of commodity prices / Plan for the rebalancing of the major world financial centres: Wall Street, the City, Switzerland, Singapore, Hong Kong and the tax havens / Inflation in the United States increases to 10% per annum / The new American President proposes organizing a new G20 summit in Frankfurt and supports the creation of a new world benchmark currency / International negotiations to set the new exchange rates / Gold is included in the basket of currencies defining the new global currency / The Dollar and the Pound are, de facto, devalued by 30% and 50% against major currencies / The Yuan is revalued by 30% and Beijing accepts its full convertibility by 2017 / Victories by National-Europeanist leaders in several EU countries / EU-Russian reconciliation over the future of the Ukraine and the Caucasus countries / Creation of the South American Union on the initiative of Brazil, Venezuela, Peru and Argentina, creation of a common currency planned for 2017 / Washington blocks all aid to Israel following a new housing project in East Jerusalem causing a political crisis in Tel Aviv and the election of a Prime Minister from the new party "One Peace & Two States Now" / Sweden and Denmark seek entry into the Eurozone / The Maastricht criteria are, exceptionally, relaxed until

---

[179] We suggest "Global" for reasons of simplicity.

[180] Any relationship to the film of the same name is purely coincidental.

2015: Debt 70% of GDP, budget deficit 5%, and inflation 4% / France launches a major tax reform broadening the tax base and increasing the taxation of the richest 10% / The Franco-German duo sets up joint cabinet meetings every six months / The Eurozone creates its own integrated institutions for economic coordination and policy, different from those of the EU / Over 50% of Catalans vote for their independence in a referendum / Start of the process of renegotiating the Nuclear Non-Proliferation Treaty.

2014: Rapid rebalancing of currency derivatives / Under the impetus. of the G20 the IMF proposes a radical reform of financial markets and the break-up of all banks "too big to fail" / Launch of rescue plans for the economies weakened most by the crisis / Stabilization of energy prices / End of the plan rebalancing major financial centers / Global unemployment stabilizes / Wall Street and part of the U.S. military-industrial complex attempt a coup d'état in the United States at the moment of a large attack attributed to Texan independentists / Replacement of the current system of IMF Special Drawing Rights (SDRs) by the new currency / India begins negotiations to join the Asian free trade zone (ASEAN + China and Japan) / End of the visa regime between the EU and Russia / Official announcement of the integration of the entire Balkans with the EU before 2020 / Two new trans-European political forces win seats in the European Parliament: the European Democratic Front and the Alliance for the European Nation / The United Kingdom seeks to enter the Eurozone by 2017 / Taiwan announces its intention to negotiate its "return" to the "mother-land" / India prepares itself for a direct conflict with the new Pakistan Islamic government / U.S. GDP falls 30% and living standards 50% compared to 2008 / Increasing number of mass killings in the United States against a backdrop of unemployment, deprivation and decay of all public services (health, law enforcement, education, etc.) / Due to budgetary constraints, the United States stops strategic assistance to Egypt as well as to a number of allied regimes / Oil is now priced in the new global benchmark currency / European roundtable on Islam in Europe issues general recommendations for its presence in European public spaces.

2015: All major energy and raw materials global markets move to the new world benchmark currency / Conversion of all international accounts (including major banks and multinational groups) to accounts in the new global benchmark currency (non-exclusive, of course, from accounts in other currencies) / The world economy is stabilizing with average growth of 1% / End of the rise in unemployment / Resumption of world trade / GDP rising in Asia, Europe, Russia and countries producing raw materials and energy / Stabilization of U.S. GDP (at least 20% compared to 2008) / 30% decrease in Americans' average standard of living / Successful reform of U.S. health care, 100% coverage of the population / Successful reform of UN governance / Creation of the Asian Union bringing together China, Japan, Korea and ASEAN countries and implementation of the Pacific free trade zone (APFTZ) / Creation of the Palestinian state, including a corridor between Palestine and Gaza / Turkey and Saudi Arabia organize a major conference on the Middle East to which Iran, Syria and Israel are invited: USA, EU, Russia and China are observers / WTO negotiations are restarted on the basis of agreements between major world regions and not between States anymore / Signature of the Treaty of Controlled Nuclear Proliferation / Declaration of a state of emergency in the southern states of the United States in the face of the spread of the conflict linked to drug traffickers and Latinos' demands for autonomy / Washington announces the issue of a New Dollar worth 10% of the old one and a rise in U.S. interest rates to crush inflation / The U.S. Federal Reserve is replaced by the Central Bank of the United States comprised only of public entities / Texas begins a process of secession / Many American states authorize the use of currencies other than the U.S. Dollar / NATO becomes the Euro-American Alliance incorporating Russia / EU adopts a law for the genetic fingerprinting of all its citizens in the fight against illegal immigration / The European Parliament decides to instigate its own validation of key positions in the Community bureaucracy / The European Parliament launches a broad public debate on the geographical location of European institutions / France decides, by referendum, on the largest territorial reorganization since the 1789 Revolution - Twelve provinces are created and central government services (State Council, Court of Auditors, Economic and Social Council) are shared between seven cities (Paris, Strasbourg, Lille, Toulouse, Marseilles, Lyon, Nice) / Deadly epidemic in the United States related to the intensive use of GMOs.

2016: The United States withdraws from most of its military bases in the world except Latin America and the Persian Gulf States / 90% of Russian nuclear missiles moved to the country's Southern and Eastern borders / The Ukraine becomes a federation of two autonomous. States separated by the Dnieper / Mass exodus of economic refugees from Africa to Europe, which leads to the creation of the European Security and Defence fleet in the Mediterranean merging the nucleus of the French, Italian, Spanish and Greek navies / EU average living standards fall 10% compared to 2006 / U.S. President re-elected on a platform of a new multipolar world order and re-industrialization of the United States / World trade has fallen 30% from 2008 levels / EU offers a 100 Billion Euro loan to the United States at zero interest rate, ironically called « ShallMar », to upgrade infrastructure and reduce reliance on GMOs and hormones in food / In Europe pensions are reduced 20% / China faces increasing pollution due to growing domestic demand / The World Summit on the Environment co-hosted in the Azores by the EU, the Latin American Union and Africa leads to a global plan to reduce world pollution 50% by 2030.

2017: Saudi Arabia and Turkey launch the MOGV "Middle-East High Speed" rail project: Syria, Iraq, Egypt, Israel, Palestine, the Lebanon and Iran are candidates to join the MOGV consortium / Former Al Qaeda operatives establish a political party in Saudi Arabia winning seats in Parliament in Jeddah / Iran announces it has five nuclear weapons - Israel admits to owning 50 / Victories by xenophobic nationalist parties in many EU countries / China, Japan, South Korea and ASEAN countries announce the creation of the Asian Union / Taiwan formalizes its unification with the People's Republic of China on the Hong Kong model / India receives the statute of an associate country of the Asian Union / Growing nuclear threats from Pakistan vis-à-vis India / California and Washington suggest merging with the Asian free trade zone / The United States/Mexico border dispute leads to a new statute for New Mexico, Arizona, California and Texas which become States associated with the federation of the United States (bilingual, special customs status with Mexico, etc.) / Opening of the overnight Brussels-Moscow TGV rail link / The EU makes the WTO accept its proposed « sustainable tax » exempting all environmentally friendly produced products from customs duties / Death of the King of Belgium leading to the demise of Belgium negotiated between the Flemish and Walloons, Flemish independence, Wallonia's annexation to France and the turning of Brussels into a European district.

2018: The Yuan increasingly used on the Pacific coast of the Americas / Russia and the Eurozone sign an exchange rate agreement with the Euro-Ruble co-ordinated at parity / The Latin American Union finally embraces the whole of Latin America after the end of Columbia's opposition / The northern states of Mexico also renegotiate their relations with Mexico / Quebec launches "North America in 2020" enterprise targeting the redefinition of the subcontinent's geopolitical fabric / The Alliance for the European Nation wins 40% of the seats in the European Parliament / The EU decides to create joint consulates in the major States of the United States / EU citizens suspected of helping illegal immigrants are deprived of their social and civil rights / First cases of fatal poisoning by nanoparticles / Joint diplomatic action by Iran, Saudi Arabia, Russia and China enables the replacement of Pakistani extremist leaders, India cancels a preemptive nuclear strike at the last minute / An American's average salary is now the same as a Pole's / Europe's savings rate has increased to 20% to compensate for the sharp decline in the reimbursement of medical costs and retirement income / A referendum to be held at the same time as the 2019 European elections to decide the EU's institutional reorganization as a network of capitals instead of the Brussels-Luxembourg-Strasbourg triangle / New series of WTO multilateral agreements bringing, on European initiative, widespread social security coverage for all countries concerned.

2019: The economic crisis and global geopolitical tensions have led to the bankruptcy of 50% of international airlines and a fall in passenger traffic to levels last seen in the 1970s / European teenagers read mostly Manhuas (Chinese mangas) combining reading from right to left , from the last to the first page with titles in ideograms / Major European university networks are twinned with their Asian counterparts / Part of Yale and Harvard's campus' bought by the Marco Polo network bringing European and Chinese universities together / 2019 European Elections are held for the first time under a single electoral law for all Member States / The European Democratic Front is credited with 35% of the vote in the next European elections / Vladimir Putin announces he is retiring from all his political functions / The fifth generation of Chinese Communist leaders are preparing to take the reins of power in Beijing / The last living founder member of Al Qaeda elected president of the Saudi legislative assembly on a platform of reforming the monarchy / The EU proposes a series of five special G20 summits (Brasilia, Beijing, Washington, Paris, New Delhi) intended to lay down the international architecture in matters of environmental, monetary, economic, scientific and military governance for the next decades.

2020: The new decade begins in a context conducive to the establishment of a new lasting global governance which will allow, perhaps, the critical collective tasks such as problems of world hunger, pollution, etc. to be addressed.

The influence of a reconstruction of the international system around a global benchmark currency would be enormous and multifaceted. First of all this process would stop dead the trend which is now becoming apparent of every man for himself, and which carries the greatest risk of conflicts in the future. All the political leaders, the major economic players and bureaucracies in the world should be dragged into an unbroken series of conferences, meetings and other joint proceedings. The converse, therefore, of a system breaking up.

Then, the implementation of this new currency would impose an automatic "purge" of the "black holes" of the financial system. The major banks' balance sheets like the profits of the mafia would face the unparalleled glare of the global spotlight. The "ghost-assets" in U.S. Dollars would be doomed to be converted into the new benchmark currency, heavily devaluing them certainly, but giving them a globally recognized value [181]. The United States' huge financial imbalances would be automatically forced down because the replacement of the Dollar as the international benchmark currency would require the United States to actually support (and not via the printing press) the burden of their oil imports, Chinese

---

[181] It's better to have a lower value than no value at all, which will happen if the other path is chosen, with the collapse of the dollar and U.S. Treasury Bonds into the bargain.

manufactured goods and their military spending. Which would be the best thing that could happen to the vast majority of U.S. citizens because that would go hand in hand with a rebalancing of public and private expenditure towards individual and collective productive activities. In effect, it's not the 300 million Americans who benefit from the current Dollar system but only the small clique which has led the whole country into the subprime catastrophe and the banking crisis and which buys corrupt regimes across the globe for next to nothing. Suddenly, the cost of a dictator would become much more expensive than when one prints the cash oneself to pay for it. Obviously, that may upset some people.

Finally, the end of currency market instability of and the opportunity to calmly plan international business transactions in the medium and long term would be a significant contribution to reviving world trade which is currently in a state of complete collapse. All these elements would bring an immediate end to the dizzying rise in unemployment underway in all major areas of the world.

Last but not least, with such an objective, world leaders would impose their pace on events whilst offering world public opinion an ambitious and stimulating target. In strategy, take control of time and stimulate ones troops, it's the only key to success!

Utopian? Not really, the Eurozone is a successful example on a small-scale of such a development. And today, because of the crisis, most European countries are eager to adopt the Euro. However, a decade ago, critics of the project's "utopianism" were numerous and virtually unanimous on Wall Street and the City. Curious, isn't it, it's always the same ones.

History has more than proved that if we do not try to build constructive alternatives, the forces of disintegration and conflict prevail. Trying to perpetuate a system is to condemn oneself to be carried away by its collapse!

2. The tragic twilight of the « world before »

Sadly, the calendar of this hypothetical future is easier to develop. Here is the overview.

2010: Global economic stagnation / Direct U.S.A/EU/Asian conflict to attract the world's savings insufficient to finance growing public deficits / Inability and growing lack of will on the part of China, Japan and the oil-producing kingdoms of the Gulf to buy the mountain of U.S. Treasury Bonds created by the exponential U.S. deficit / Unveiling of the massive disguised repurchase of U.S. Treasury Bonds by the Fed / 500 billion U.S. Dollar emergency package to avoid the collapse of U.S. states and local authorities / Increasing gold purchases by central banks worldwide / Acceleration of the growth in unemployment throughout the world (20% in the United States and Europe) / Chinese growth falls below 5% / American and European governments refuse to impose further taxes and other financial charges on the richest 10% / In the United Kingdom the government is obliged to cut public sector pensions by 50% and civil servants' salaries by 20% / China continues to refuse to revalue the Yuan

2011: Further fall in world GDP following the withdrawal of liquidity provided by central banks and the inability of countries to finance new stimulus plans / G20 meetings become more and more difficult (like the Copenhagen summit), leading to meaningless press releases / Washington's refusal to organize a G20 meeting in Moscow: G20 meeting will be held in Tokyo / United States' unemployment exceeds 20% / Spreading anti-Fed and anti-Wall Street mass action / Daily migrant workers riots in China / Greece, Spain and Italy are obliged to activate a drastic austerity package under the supervision of the ECB / Demonstrations and daily strikes in major European cities / Increasing number of European referenda and regional decisions against Islam's exterior aspects (veil, burka, minaret) / In Spain unemployment reaches 30% of the working population / In the United Kingdom the government is obliged to cut public sector pensions by 50% and civil servants' salaries by 20% / In France Nicolas Sarkozy imposes the continuation of the tax shield on his reluctant party, thus preventing any budget rebalancing / Collapse of tax receipts in the United States, many States such as Texas and California refuse to remit tax receipts to the Federal Government / Growing doubts over the exact amount of United States gold reserves/ Multiplying bankruptcies of local authorities almost everywhere in the world / Major U.S. banks request a new one trillion USD rescue plan / The dollar falls a further 20% against other major currencies / United States inflation exceeds 10% / China and Japan establish a

Yen/Yuan swap facility between their central banks / Increase in anti-federal attacks in the United States perpetrated by extreme right-wing militias / Out and out NATO failure in Afghanistan – European troops withdrawn

2012: The United States announces a complete withdrawal of its troops from Afghanistan following the capture of a U.S. base by the Taliban / Growing disruption of the world economic fabric (production chains for a large number of products interrupted by the bankruptcy of key suppliers) / Return of commercial and economic blocs after the refusal to follow WTO trade rulings / Migration of environmental themes to the economic and geopolitical spheres / European threats to impose heavy customs duties on products adjudged to have a production process carrying a strong risk of pollution / Growing suspicion that the United States only holds 50% of its officially declared gold reserves / Asian embargo on U.S. agricultural products / Washington is obliged, once again, to invest one trillion USD to save the big banks from bankruptcy / The new General Motors files for bankruptcy / Further 15% fall in value of the U.S. Dollar / China and Russia, followed by Japan and the oil producing countries, announce that they will no longer hold the Pound Sterling as part of their currency reserves / The British pound falls 50% against major international currencies / The United Kingdom is obliged to organise a sale of Lloyds and RBS' assets / Putin is elected Russian President again / Obama is beaten by a Republican wishing to "keep national unity and fight domestic enemies" / Nicolas Sarkozy is re-elected French President against a backdrop of massive fraud / The Northern League receives 60% of the votes cast in Northern Italy and demands a referendum on the partition of Italy / The Catalans announce unilateral independence / Scotland and Wales demand the creation of a British federal state / The IRA takes up arms again in Northern Ireland / Attempted assassination of the Chairman of the U.S. Federal Reserve / China continues to keep the Yuan/Dollar peg - Growing monetary tensions with ASEAN countries

2013: Victory of Nationalist-Europeanist leaders in many EU countries / Re-establishment of good relations between the EU and Russia over the future of the Ukraine and the Caucasus countries / Acceleration of the integration of the Union of South American Nations (UNASUR) on the initiative of Brazil, Venezuela, Peru and Argentina: common currency expected in 2017 / Failure of the holding of a BRIC-EU summit at Sochi due to American pressure / U.S. inflation rises to 20% per annum / Chrysler is sold by Fiat to a Chinese auto builder for a symbolic one USD / Sweden and Denmark request Eurozone membership / The Maastricht criteria are modified: debt at 80% of GDP, budget deficit at 7% - The Euro falls 20% against the Yuan, the Real and the Australian Dollar / France sinks into long term political instability / Germany remains the only major country not to succumb to a wave of electoral xenophobia / Anti-gipsy purges increase in Eastern Europe /

The Eurozone creates its own integrated institutions for economic and political coordination, separate from those of the EU / Deadly attack on Goldman Sachs' New York headquarters / Strong growth in crime in Europe as well as the United States / In Amsterdam, Copenhagen and Tokyo pensioners demonstrate violently over the bankruptcy of pension funds / Many states insist, in vain, on the repatriation of their gold reserves held in New York and London / Suspicion that the reserves in question are not available / Gold trades at $3,000 oz

2014: End of the visa system between the EU and Russia / European celebration in Sarajevo in July 2014 not leading to any agreement on Balkan integration / Two new trans-European political forces join the European Parliament: the European Democratic Front and the Alliance for a European Nation / First deportations of Muslim fundamentalists from France and the Netherlands / Taiwan announces its intention to negotiate its "return" to the "mother-land" / India prepares itself for direct conflict with the new Pakistan Islamic power / 30% fall in U.S. GDP and a 50% fall in the standard of living compared to 2008 / Increasing number of collective killings in the United States in a context of unemployment, shortages and the breakdown in public services (health, police, education) / Due to budget constraints the United States ends strategic aid to Egypt as well as a number of allied regimes / Japan faces an unprecedented crime wave / Wave of anti-Chinese attacks in Japan / Terrorism for independence increases in Europe (Corsica, the Basque country, Catalonia, Flanders, Scotland, Northern Ireland, the Carpathian countries, Northern Italy) / China announces the end of the Yuan/Dollar peg and, simultaneously, the creation of a new pan-Asian currency joining the Yuan, the Yen and all the ASEAN currencies / Continuing collapse of the U.S. Dollar / Growing chronic instability on all markets (currencies, commodities, stocks, bonds)

2015: Israel, in the middle of a full economic crisis, attacks Iranian nuclear installations / Immediate military response from all Arab and Muslim countries / Turkey supports the anti-Israel front and officially announces the abandonment of its EU integration project / Washington decides to send troops to help defend Israel / The U.S. Dollar falls a further 30% against major world currencies when China suddenly announces free convertibility of the Yuan for all transactions with Japan and ASEAN countries, as well as the sale of 500 billion USD worth of U.S. Treasury Bonds / The G20, under Chinese and Saudi Arabian pressure, demands that Israel returns to its 1967 borders and the immediate creation of a Palestinian state / One million Israeli citizens emigrate to Europe, the United States, Canada and Australia / Increasing shortages of food, medicines, spare parts and energy in many parts of the world / Declaration of a state of emergency in the Southern States of the United States against a backdrop of an extension of the conflict related to drug traffickers and Latinos separatist claims / Washington announces

144

the issue of a new Dollar worth 10% of the old one / Texas starts a process of secession / Many American states authorise the use of currencies other than the U.S. Dollar / The last U.S. troops leave Europe and NATO becomes the Euro-American Alliance incorporating Russia / The EU adopts a law of genetic fingerprinting for all its citizens in the fight against clandestine immigration / A popular European proposal, confirmed by the European Commission, plans prohibiting the construction of any further mosques on EU territory / The United Kingdom requests entry into the Eurozone by 2020 / The world economy suffers a new 10% recession / Oil is now priced in gold / Hereinon gold is quoted in Euros and in the common Asian currency - Average price for the year: 2,000 Euros an ounce

2016: Attempt by the United States to create a Bolivian Union based around Columbia, opening the way to the start of a regional military conflict / The United States withdraws from the majority of its military bases in the world, with the exception of Latin America and the Persian Gulf States / Transfer of 90% of Russian nuclear missiles to the country's Southern and Eastern borders / The Ukraine becomes a federation of two independent states separated by the Dnieper river / Massive exodus of economic refugees from Africa to Europe leading to the creation of a European security and defence fleet in the Mediterranean merging the nucleus of the French, Italian, Spanish and Greek navies / Increasing number of anti-Muslim incidents in Europe / 20% fall in EU living standards / Election of a new American President on an isolationist programme / World trade has fallen 50% from 2008 levels / Hunger riots increase in the United States / In Europe pensions are halved / China executes a huge number of rioters to contain an unprecedented wave of public violence / A new World Summit on the Environment organised by the European Union attracts none of the major powers apart from Russia and Brazil / The international watchdog on anti-Semitism identifies the United States as the leading country for the number and gravity of anti-Semitic acts / Serbia and Montenegro request admission to the Russian Federation / The chief prosecutor of the European Court of Justice is assassinated after a resounding success in a case concerning the mafia's rise in power in major European banks / Beijing declares a state of emergency in all its outlying provinces (Tibet, XinKiang, Inner Mongolia) in the face of social and ethnic riots / Deadly epidemic related to the intensive usee of GMOs in Latin America.

2017: Saudi Arabia signs a defence agreement with China / American rebuff and coup d'état in Jeddah / Iran, Iraq, China, the U.S.A and the Gulf States start a regional conflict / Due to lack of investment and because of regional crises, world oil production capacity collapses and the oil price doubles / Xenophobe nationalist parties win victories in numerous European countries / China, Japan, South Korea and ASEAN countries announce the creation of the Asian Union / Taiwan formalises its unification with the People's Republic of China based on the Hong Kong model / India receives the status of an Asian Union associate country / Growing nuclear threats from Pakistan against India / The Asian Union reaches a preferential customs agreement with California and Washington State / The conflict on the U.S./Mexican border leads to a new status for New Mexico, Arizona, California and Texas which become States associated with the Federation of the United States / Inauguration of the last section of track for the Brussels-Moscow overnight TGV / The EU announces a 200% customs tariff on any product manufactured in a "non sustainable" manner, excluding Russia and Latin America / China declares an embargo on all "rare earths" destined for the EU / The Eurabia terrorist group claims responsibility for the assassination of the President of the European Commission / For its 30th anniversary the Erasmus programme is brought to a close without a successor due to lack of funds / Death of the King of Belgium followed by a unilateral declaration of Flemish independence / Brussels occupied by Flemish militia / Temporary transfer of the European Parliament to Strasbourg

2018: Increasing use of the Yuan on the Americas' Pacific coast / Russia and the Eurozone sign an agreement for coordinated parity between the Euro and Ruble / Russia obtains a watching role over the affairs of the Baltic States from the European Union / The conflict in the North of Latin America draws in all Central America / An imploded Mexico is no longer really a State / Quebec launches the initiative "North America 2020" attempting to redefine the geopolitical fabric of the sub-continent / The Alliance for the European Nation wins 40% of the seats in the European Parliament / The EU decides to open embassies in the major States of the United States / European citizens suspected of helping illegal immigrants are stripped of their social benefits and civic rights / First cases of deadly poisoning from nanoparticles / India launches a preemptive nuclear strike on Pakistan's nuclear installations: Chinese neutrality and American and European indifference / Skirmishes between Chinese and European troops in Africa increase / The average U.S. salary is now the same as the Chinese / The rate of savings in Europe has risen to 30% to compensate for the collapse in reimbursement of health charges and retirement income / Successful referendum on the issue of the unification of Wallonia with France – Brutal intervention by the Eurocorps to establish peace in Brussels and clear the European Parliament buildings

2019: The economic crisis and worldwide geopolitical tensions have caused the bankruptcy of 50% of the international airlines with passenger traffic levels falling to those of the 1970s / EU importation of Mangas (Japanese comics) and Manhuas (Chinese comics), reading from right to left from the last to the first page and with ideogram titles prohibited / University exchanges worldwide are in freefall, restricted to each large geopolitical bloc / The Alliance for the European Nation announces that if it wins the next European elections it will install an electronic surveillance barrier the length of the Union's borders and will authorize shooting as a legitimate defence to repel illegal immigrants / Large-scale deportations of fundamentalist Muslims from Europe / All private U.S. universities are nationalised to prevent their bankruptcy / The U.S. army threatens a military coup d'état if the next President, selected in the 2020 elections, proves himself incapable of re-establishing the United States to its former self territorially / The European Democratic Front is credited with winning 30% of the votes at the next European elections, but demands that Latin American and African observers be sent to ensure the legality of the voting process / The new Chinese President announces that China and the Asian Union are demanding that Russia should open Siberia to the free settlement of their citizens / Vladimir Putin suspends the Russian Constitution and declares a state of emergency in the face of this Chinese claim / The last living founder member of Al-Qaida ends a round of conferences in the Persian Gulf States / Military budgets are growing strongly throughout the world / The U.S. navy cruises off Brazilian and Argentinean ports to force the signature of an agreement of free exchange between the Latin American Union and the United States / Average life expectancy in the United States falls by five years compared to 2009

2020...: The beginning of another decade, in the worst possible world context since the 1930s

In conclusion, if this book has enabled the reader to take off the blinkers which our contemptible elite try to keep over our eyes to box in our ability to anticipate the near future, especially when raising new issues, then I think it has been worthwhile writing it. If it has given him a better understanding of the historical importance of the crisis in progress, the magnitude of the changes that will characterize the world after the crisis and allow the reader to better prepare for it, then I know it was necessary to write it. And if it leads in some small way to help the French and Europeans to collectively face the challenges of the 2010-2020 decade, thus adding crucial force to divert world history from a tragic course, then I am convinced that it was necessary to write it.

In this regard, I cannot help but add three final recommendations:

- Don't listen to the elite when they say that you, citizens or people cannot change anything. Major historical trends can no longer, in effect, be stopped, no more than one can block the course of a river, but they can be controlled, restricted and sometimes diverted; considerably if it is done in time because the key to history is always the time factor.

- With the crisis and its effects before our very eyes, think twice from now on before supporting any particular political leader. The crisis has shown that politics are essential, especially when things go wrong. So keep in mind that the years ahead need European leaders who understand their own people, of course, but also other people whose destiny is now linked to ours in this world after the crisis where Chinese, Indian, Russian, American and European supertankers cruise! Check, like they did a century ago for the ability to read and write, that they have an understanding of at least one other language and that they belong to the twenty-first century and its multi-polarity. It's little to ask, but in the current context it would be a giant step forward.

- In confronting the dangers of history we can overcome them, not by allowing them to be lulled by gentle illusions or wallowing in egocentric discussions. In these cases, we end up by collectively and individually paying a terrible cost.

The success of the European Community project launched after the Second World War was particularly due to an historically innovative choice made by the generation of "Founding Fathers" of the EU: " Limit the power" that had led Europeans on the road to suicide twice in succession and rebuild the European international order on a rationale of dialogue, compromise, sharing the treasures and the problems, the ups and downs. It's the suppression of power, especially by the "large Member States", which has gradually helped the Community project to advance. A similar ambition, conceived as a sharing of experiences with the rest of the world, must inspire the EU's international action in the decades to come, that is to say:

- Become the most influential global player while refusing to try and be the most powerful.

- Inhibit our own power abroad to demonstrate that we can nevertheless influence the course of events for the better and lead our partners in a common direction.

It's neither a matter of a political utopia here (or in any case no more utopian than the idea of the EU founders over 50 years ago), nor of a theoretical prior assumption (because one can see every day how the use of power in the complex world of the twenty-first century is a dangerous and unpredictable option[182]). It's the assertion that the world after the crisis, globalized but fragmented between rival blocs, interconnected, densely populated, subject to growing dangers coming into focus (climate risks, health risks, etc.), cannot be managed like the world was in previous centuries. It's not so much the enemies who are the twenty-first century threats, but the common problems for which we do not supply the means to find common solutions. Based on this analysis, one can only innovate in terms of international relations and build a new global governance, or continue as if nothing had changed and make future generations pay a terrible price.

This world after the crisis can certainly be very much more ours, we Europeans, than before the crisis, if we refer to the principles and diversity that may distinguish it, rather than the colour of those who are its elite. In any case the Europeans now need to make the choice of audacity and innovation. Exemplarity being the only lasting historical force, it's our move!

---

[182] The United States is falling apart before our very eyes, especially because such an act goes almost exclusively with classic imperial power, that of brute force.

Contents

Réalisation PAO :
Kerozen
116, bd de la République - 78400 Chatou
www.kerozen-concept .com

Achevé d'imprimer par :
Drukarnia PANDA
ul. Paczkowska 26
50-503 Wrocław - Pologne

Dépôt légal : Décembre 2010